ALMOST *Eden*

All the Best!
Kim Bullgraw

ALMOST *Eden*

Designing Gardens in Relation to Creation

KIM BURGSMA

ALMOST EDEN: DESIGNING GARDENS IN RELATION TO CREATION

Scripture taken from the HOLY BIBLE, NEW INTERNATIONAL VERSION®. Copyright © 1973, 1978, 1984 International Bible Society. Used by permission of Zondervan. All rights reserved.

Scripture quotations are taken from the Holy Bible, New Living Translation, copyright ©1996, 2004, 2007 by Tyndale House Foundation. Used by permission of Tyndale House Publishers, Inc., Carol Stream, Illinois 60188. All rights reserved.

Photography by Holly Maria Burgsma and Kim Burgsma with the exception of page 40, which is credited to Danielle Burgsma.

Photography Editor: Holly Burgsma Photography, www.hollyburgsmaphotography.com.

Cover image taken from Butchart Gardens, Central Saanich BC

Editors: Carol Ann Hiemstra & Darinka Korosec

ISBN: 978-1-77069-243-5

Printed in Canada

Word Alive Press
131 Cordite Road, Winnipeg, MB R3W 1S1
www.wordalivepress.ca

WORD ALIVE PRESS
Just Write!

Library and Archives Canada Cataloguing in Publication

Burgsma, Kim
Almost Eden / Kim Burgsma.

ISBN 978-1-77069-243-5

1. Gardening--Religious aspects--Christianity. 2. Gardens--
Religious aspects--Christianity. I. Title.

BV4596.G36B87 2011   242'.68   C2011-900978-1

"Almost Eden *is a real treat. The reader enjoys a message delivered straight from Kim's heart while benefiting from her considerable experience on a very practical level. The photographs alone are worth the price of the book.*

Whether you indulge in the experience of gardening with both knees and hands or enjoy armchair gardening this book provides a wealth of inspiration."

Mark Cullen

Endorsement

To my father who now is in heaven who at the springtime of my life and the winter of his, left me with three simple yet powerful words of faith, "God is good". If he could see me today I believe his heart would swell with pride. Not because of who I am or what I have become, but because I have chosen to follow the God of my father.

Dedication

TABLE OF CONTENTS

I'd like to thank so many people who helped in some way to make this book possible. To Hugh, the man who has loved and encouraged me for over half my life. Without your prodding and passionate belief in me this book would have never been written. I love you more each day. To Mom and Dad who believe, as all great parents should, that their daughter can do anything. To my firstborn Robin who decided, with excited certainty, that my book would make it onto store shelves. To Jordan who loves words as much as I do. I see a novel in your future. To my daughter Holly, who has grown into my friend and shares my love of all things beautiful. You will do well in your creative field. To Danielle, Michelle, and Phil, who, too often, had to patiently listen to my obsession with my book. Each one of you has been a blessing in my life. To Jane, my true soul sister, who read every word and thought they were all wonderful. I think if I wrote a 500-page book on mud you still would have said it was great. To Darinka, my dear friend with gifts of her own yet to be shared. To Jeremy, I know God has amazing things in store for you. To Joannie, Laurie, Cindy, Claudette, Gil, and Stephen, who encouraged me and kept my secret. To Eleanor, who is a wealth of information and encouragement. To Nicky Lambert it was fun working with you. Thanks for trusting me. To Don Pape who was never too busy to help. You are truly the kindest person I've met in the industry. Thanks to Dr. Feenstra who willingly offered advice. To Martin Quinn and Catherine Macleod for believing in my work enough to write the foreword. It's so nice to be associated with such like-minded horticulturalists. To Mark Cullen, Canada's King of Horticulture, for his support and kind words. To Carol Ann Hiemstra, your editing advice was invaluable, and Erin Wilson of Green Dot Design who made my book so presentable. Thanks to everyone at Word Alive Press, particularly Caroline Schmidt for answering my constant questions and Nikki Braun whose artistic eye was responsible for the final layout. And to everyone at The Word Guild, you have taught me so much.

Thanks to everyone who invited Holly and I into your public gardens and private oasis. Your gardens are beautiful and I am grateful that you allowed me to share them with others.

Acknowledgements

Growing where we are planted, the natural way.

Take Kim's hand on a gardening journey and learn how she views native plants in a naturalized garden. The work is a labyrinth of ideas, plant attributes and combinations through the eye's of a creative, environmentally conscious Landscape Designer. Whether her readers' garden gate is secular or sacred, Kim's approach to garden design motivates readers to think deeply about what they are doing -- when and how. Her list of plants and gardening schedule are alone worth the read.

Kim begins at the beginning with soil, sand, silt and clay (earth) and shows how pH levels affect plant growth. To prepare a garden Kim weighs the alternatives of chemical and organic methods of fertilizing, weed and pest control, composting and watering. How to use compost is a central concern.

Next Kim invites her readers to look up at trees and considers how to best live with them. She asks elemental questions like: is the appropriate tree in its appropriate place? She concludes that being involved in community Arbor Days is a good starting point for natural garden lovers.

Equipped with a basic knowledge of soils and trees, Kim urges environmental stewards to observe the changing seasons. Deceptively asleep or dormant, the earth in winter allows land stewards to observe its bones or structure. In winter, the eye can see various plant forms and shapes and consider residential or inspirational objects of art.

In spring, the garden inspires ideas. Land stewards have the capacity to work in tandem with nature's annual and perennial presentations. As summer and fall unfold they create opportunities for infinite plays of color combinations and planting styles, as diverse as each climate, microclimate and participant. Even night time is garden time in Kim's environmental scope.

Her scope embraces the wonders of co-creation and points to ways even the plant market attempts to work in harmony with nature. How do new plants show up in nurseries each spring? Kim affirms the work of hybridizers who spot the emergence of new plants as well as the many other specialists who are learning to work with plant life in the global ecosystem.

Martin Quinn and
Catherine Macleod
Goderich, Ontario
2011
Co-Authors of Grass Scapes:
Gardening with Ornamental
Grasses

13

Foreword

Appreciate Natural Gardens

"See how the lilies of the field grow.

They do not labor or spin.

Yet I tell you that not even Solomon in

all his splendor was dressed like one of these."

Matthew 6:28b-29 NIV

The most amazing gardens are not created by an acclaimed landscape architect, nor are they maintained by a famous horticulturalist. The supreme landscape architect is, was, and always will be God, who created all things in the heavens and the earth. The most majestic gardens can be found in the rainforest and wilderness where God is not only the creator, but also the sole maintainer. There has never been a person who could recreate the magnificent beauty God has lavished on this earth— no waterfall so mighty, no forest so remarkable, no rockscape so imposing, no garden so impressive.

Butchart Gardens, Central Saanich BC

Native and Naturalized Gardens

Native gardens only contain plants that are indigenous to their particular geographical location. These gardens are self-sustaining and very hardy. Native plants thrive in their home environment because God planted them in their ideal growing conditions. They exist in the perfect light, moisture, soil, and nutrient conditions made just for a particular plant or grouping of plants.

Naturalized gardens differ from native gardens in that naturalized gardens may have plants that are not indigenous to the local geographical area.

Naturalized gardens are found not only in rainforests and remote mountain or desert regions, but also in woodlands, swamps, and roadside ditches close to our homes. Naturalized means simply that the garden was not intentionally planted by humankind. Soil moved from one location to another may bring with it seeds or root fragments that become trees and plants in their new site. Seeds from nearby plants and trees have been carried by wind, birds, animals, and people. Each seed is designed to naturalize in one way or another. A seed from a milkweed has a fluffy wing on it. This bit of fluff will be picked up by the wind and floated off to a new location to begin

a new plant. Various nuts are attractive to creatures such as squirrels. The squirrels will transport and bury the nuts to caches they make to provide for their winter dietary needs. Not all of these will be eaten, nor will all be found back by the squirrel. These remaining nuts, or seeds, will transform into saplings the following season. Birds will eat seeds and berries from a wide variety of plants. Many of these seeds will remain intact within the digestive system and the bird will deposit them, often far from where they first grew. The added benefit of such seeds is that they are planted complete with fertilizer! Other seeds have rough edges, or sticky prickles. These

Appreciate Natural Gardens

Milner Gardens and Woodland,
Qualicum Beach BC

seeds are naturalized when they stick to the fur of animals, or onto our clothes and shoes. They then fall or are rubbed off in another location. Plants with such seeds can also end up growing far from their initial site.

Throughout history, explorers and settlers have brought plant material from one continent to another for culinary, medicinal, and decorative purposes. Many of these plants have escaped from their initial planting sites and have naturalized in their new continent. There are, therefore, very few truly pristine native gardens. The majority of our world's native gardens have, over the centuries, become naturalized gardens with a mix of native and naturalized plant material. The majority of plant introductions into nonnative sites have been a blessing of diversity and interest.

Naturalizing also happens within our cultivated home gardens. Often this can be that little bit of serendipity when a lone flower surprises us where we least expected to see it. It may be a plant transported from another part of our garden, or perhaps a new introduction from our neighbor's back yard.

Conserving Native Gardens

Native gardens are in danger when their ideal natural environment is disturbed in some manner. When a forest is clear-cut, the vegetation below will disappear because their ideal light conditions have been drastically altered. Plants that were formerly in full shade are now exposed to full sunlight. Life-sustaining moisture now quickly evaporates, leaving the native plants parched and thirsty. The fallen debris the trees once provided is no longer there to decay and fertilize the ground. When wetlands are drained to provide increased space for urban or agricultural development, plants that only exist in wet, damp conditions die.

The introduction of nonnative, invasive types of ornamental, medicinal, and culinary plants into our home gardens has also resulted in changes to natural environments. Species seeds deposited by wind and creatures have allowed invasive plants to grow and spread quickly to nearby natural environments. Excess plants from aquariums and water gardens that are inappropriately disposed of have made their way into our

Milner Gardens and Woodland,
Qualicum Beach BC

streams, rivers, and lakes. Aquatic invasive plants spread further into our water systems when they become entangled on the propellers of boats that travel through various waterways. Species are labeled "invasive" due to the following characteristics:

- ability to flourish in a wide variety of habitats
- abundant seed production
- ability to propagate vegetatively
- absence of pests or pathogens
- highly successful in seed dispersal, germination, and colonization
- ability to over-run native species
- difficult and costly to remove or control

When natural environments are drastically altered, we not only lose the native plants but birds, insects, and other creatures, move elsewhere to find suitable food and habitation. For some species there is no suitable habitat nearby. Such displacement of God's creatures results in the extinction of various species.

We are responsible for the preservation of healthy ecosystems. God gave us that responsibility in the Garden of Eden. We need to be increasingly mindful of how we use the resources available to us, and to

The Governors House Gardens, Victoria BC

Appreciate Natural Gardens

Dogwood (*Cornus alternifolia*)

want specific native plants in your garden, purchase them from ethical nurseries that grow their own plants rather than harvesting them from the wild. Purchase products made from sustainable resources whenever possible. Strive to be chemical free to prevent excess and residual poisons from leaching into our water tables. All of these efforts will benefit our natural environment.

Woodland Gardens

A walk through the woods will reveal something different each month of the year. Fresh, green growth on the trees in spring will become a kaleidoscope of foliage in the fall. Blossoms from dogwood *(Cornus florida)*, wild apple *(Malus species)*, and choke cherry *(Prunus virginiana)* trees will turn into black and red fruit that feeds wildlife in the winter. After blanketing a forest floor with white flowers in May, wakerobin *(Trillium grandiflorum)*, give way to trout lily *(Erythronium)* and lady's slipper orchid *(Cypripedium calceolus)* flowers. Red berries from false Solomon's seal *(Smilax racemosa)*, baneberry *(Actaea rubra)*, and jack-in-the-pulpits *(Arisaema triphyllum)*, will follow when the yellow blossoms fall. Deep green mosses and contorted, textured funguses inhabit the forest all the year through.

be conscious of what we purchase and how it is packaged. It is necessary to be mindful of how our consumerist needs and desires are balanced with environmental needs. There are things that we can do to help slow down the disappearance of our natural environments. We can educate ourselves on what plants are considered invasive in our area and not purchase or plant them in our gardens. Eliminate invasive plants from your cultivated gardens by digging them out and burning them.

When disposing of excess water garden and aquarium plants, be sure to pour out the water and plants on dry ground so that plants cannot take root again. Express your views to nurseries and garden centers who sell plants that can spread to our wilderness areas. Customer feedback can have a big impact on products that are sold. Although it may be tempting, do not dig up native plants from the wild; leave their flowers where they are situated so they may go to seed and continue to naturalize. If you

White Trillium (*Trillium grandiflorum*), Wild Ginger (*Asarum europaeum*), Solomons Seal (*Smilax racemosa*)
Trout Lily (*Erythronium americanum*), Fritillary (*Fritillaria meleagris*), Lady's Slipper Orchid (*Cypripedium caleolus*)
Ox-eye Daisy (*Chrysanthemum leucanthemum*), Jack in the Pulpit (*Arisaema triphyllum*), Baneberry (*Actaea rubra*)

Appreciate Natural Gardens

The forest is also a great place for foragers. Tender fiddleheads, ferns that are just beginning to emerge, make a tasty side dish and are plentiful in early spring. Edible wild mushrooms abound in all seasons. Wild grape vines *(Vitis species)*, elderberry *(Sambuccus canadensis)*, and a variety of other delectable delights can be found in woodlands. It is essential to pick only what you know to be plentiful, and not in danger of becoming scarce due to foraging. Know what is edible, since some varieties of mushrooms and berries can cause stomach upset or poisoning. Many berries are sour to eat, but are wonderful once made into juice, jams, or pies. Many good field guides are available to assist you in properly identifying plant species. It's a good idea to take one into the woods with you when you first begin to pick its bounty.

Roadside Gardens

We cannot drive down any road without seeing wildflowers, cattails, and tall, fluffy grasses or shrubs and trees presenting us with colorful foliage, twigs, and blossoms. The toughest of the tough plants exist on roadsides. Wildflowers scattered directly beside the road have to contend with very gravelly soil, summer's heat radiating from asphalt, and salt spray from roads in wintertime. A little further down on the roadside, plants in the ditches have to deal with continually wet conditions and soggy roots. Our pampered garden plants would never put up with such conditions. Nor would these tough roadside plants put up with being pampered in our gardens. As a result, we get to enjoy

different plants when we go for a roadside walk than when we take a stroll in our gardens. Many municipalities keep our roadsides "tidy" by regularly cutting back long grasses growing in the ditches. This is often necessary to prevent tree seedlings from growing and obstructing drivers' sightlines as well as preventing trees from becoming a hazard to overhead wires. The negative side is that they are not selective in their cutting and often shear back lovely wildflowers before we have enjoyed their blossoms. Each spring for many years, I would call my municipality's roads department and ask that they not cut in front of my home property. You see, the roadside next to my home was so naturalized with orange daylily *(Hemerocallis),* that the display was absolutely stunning for several weeks each summer. To my dismay, not two weeks after we moved from our home, the ditches were cut, right before the daylilies were to flower. We need to educate

The Governors House Gardens, Victoria BC

Appreciate Natural Gardens

others to appreciate the simple beauty that is displayed in underappreciated locations.

Wetland Gardens

A wetland is never completely quiet, yet it is a peaceful place. When I think of a wetland, the first sense that awakens in me is the sounds that emanate from it. The song of birds, murmurings of frogs, hum of dragonflies' wings and the call of various creatures fills the air. The life teeming inside serenades each hour of the day. Second only to the rainforest, wetlands are home to the most diverse wildlife in terrestrial habitat. While we don't all live close to acres of marshlands, miles of lakefront, or near estuaries and floodplains, many of us have creeks, swamps, ponds, and riversides nearby. These little bits of wetland host many of the same plants and creatures that larger wetlands do.

Downy tufts of pussywillows *(Salix gracilistyla)*, furry spikes of cattails *(Typha species)*, velvety milkweed pods *(Asclepias incarnate)*, soft plumes of swamp grass as well as sunny marsh marigolds *(Caltha palustris)*, and wildflowers delight us. In addition, they also provide food and shelter for amphibians, fowl, and insects.

Wetlands are highly efficient water purifiers and are responsible for clean drinking water. Sediment and impurities are removed from water as it percolates through the different layers in the wetland, and then into our ground water tables, lakes and rivers. The abundance of clean drinking water that we have grown accustomed to is in decline due to urban sprawl which has edged out large portions of our wetlands.

Wetlands not only offer wonderful sounds and sights, but are places of great opportunity for activity. There is so much to do within a wetland for people of all ages. They provide places for solitary enjoyment, family

The Governors House Gardens, Victoria BC

The Governors House Gardens, Victoria BC

expeditions, and serious male bonding. Hunters look forward to duck hunting season and anglers can find something to fish for all year round. Whether you enjoy kayaking or canoeing a river, swimming in lakes or ponds, bird watching or just mucking through ankle high water in rubber boots scooping up salamanders and frogs, a visit to your local wetland is always a pleasure.

The wonderful thing about native and naturalized gardens is that anyone can enjoy them. No one is responsible for buying expensive plants, tilling the soil, or spending hours in garden maintenance. No additions of water or fertilizers are necessary. Such gardens exist to glorify God and are present for our enjoyment. And they are everywhere! *"The desert and the parched land will be glad; the wilderness will rejoice and blossom. Like the crocus, it will burst into bloom; it will rejoice greatly and shout for joy"* (Isaiah 35:1, 2a NIV). Let us be ever diligent about preserving these beautiful places.

Butchart Gardens, Central Saanich BC

Appreciate Natural Gardens

RESPECTFULLY TEND THE EARTH

"He makes grass grow for the cattle, and plants

for man to cultivate—bringing forth food from the earth:

wine that gladdens the heart of man, oil to make his face shine,

and bread that sustains his heart."

Psalm 104:14, 15 NIV

Butchart Gardens, Central Saanich BC

Before Adam was created, the Bible speaks of the need for someone to cultivate the garden. When God placed Adam in the Garden of Eden, he gave him the responsibility of caring for it and tending it. In the garden everything worked together to enrich the soil so it could feed its plants. Animals and insects worked in balance with each other. And weeds didn't seem to exist at all.

We no longer live in this perfect garden, but we are still called to tend the earth. When we do this, we discover that God's original design of balance and interplay between organisms continues to exist. It's up to us to care for the elements that make up today's gardens.

Kitty Coleman Woodland Gardens, Victoria BC

Soil

We need a regular supply of nutritious food and water for our bodies to be healthy and well. When we eat improperly it allows an avenue for viruses and bacteria to set up shop in our bodies and cause us to be sick. When we eat poorly for a lifetime, serious diseases such as diabetes, heart disease, and some cancers can attack our bodies and even kill us. Our bodies are only as good as what we put into them; so it is for plants as well. Plants can only thrive and survive in soils that provide enough nutrients, oxygen, and moisture on a regular basis. A soil which lacks

even one of these elements is a soil where plants will struggle to grow. When plants are struggling to survive, insects, bacteria, and viruses are more easily able to attack, thus stunting the plant's growth and even killing the plant. Building up your garden soil is the most important investment of both time and money to be made in your garden. Your soil needs to be in tip-top shape prior to planting and will need attention on a regular basis to make up for plants naturally depleting its nutrients. So before you purchase beautiful, expensive plants, make sure your soil will support them.

It is important to assess your garden soil before you begin to garden. If you are gardening in an area near a dump site, chemical factory, or other activities which could affect it, you should have your soil professionally analyzed right away. This is particularly important if you plan to grow plants for food. However, it is usually sufficient to analyze your soil yourself by feeling it, watching how quickly or slowly water moves through it, and by looking at the surrounding area's trees, plants, and buildings. A good garden soil will be dark in color and be pH neutral. If a portion of soil is squeezed into a ball it should not quickly crumble apart nor stay compacted in a tight ball. Not many people are blessed

with an ideal soil composition to start with, but ideal soil can be made over a period of time. If there is only an inch or two of topsoil where you are planning your garden, you will need to remove a foot or two of the subsoil and replace it with loam-rich topsoil.

Sand

Sandy soils are dark in color and light in weight. The advantages of having a sandy soil base is that it heats up quickly, thus allowing you to garden early in the spring and late into the fall. Sandy soils are light and easy to dig in and weeds pull out without effort. Water drains easily through the soil and oxygen is in plentiful supply. The disadvantage of sandy soils is that, since water passes through the soil easily, more frequent waterings are necessary. It also means that nutrients pass quickly through the soil along with the water.

When compressing moist sandy soil in your hand, it will rapidly fall apart when you open your hand and will have a gritty feel to it. Sandy soils are one of the easiest soils to amend. A generous portion of compost, leaf mould, peat moss, and manure will help the soil to gain more substance and thus hold water better and add nutrients necessary for optimal plant growth and vigor.

Silt

Silt soils hold water better than sandy soils and are fairly rich in nutrients. Unfortunately, silty soils can be rather heavy in weight and tightly compacted, therefore digging in the soil can be a chore. Water passes through such soil slowly, thus leaving a risk of root rot for plants standing in waterlogged conditions. When the soil dries, it is fine and can be dusty. Silt soil feels silky between the fingers when wet and forms a ball that holds its shape when moist and compressed. Additions of compost, leaf mold, peat moss, and manure will help to add larger soil particles and therefore better drainage capabilities, improved oxygen circulation, and lighter weight soil.

Clay

Clay soils are light in color and very heavy in weight. Clay is rich in nutrients and holds moisture well,

Glendale Gardens, Victoria BC

meaning there will be less frequent waterings when the weather is hot. Unfortunately, that's about the only blessing it affords a gardener. Clay takes a long time to heat up and therefore delays the ability to garden for some time in spring. Clay holds water and does not provide sufficient oxygen necessary to maintain healthy roots. Root rot is common in clay soils. Clay can be back breaking to dig in and weeds take great effort to extract from clay. The soil's surface bakes in the sun and becomes hard when dry, leaving cracks and making it difficult for water to penetrate. Clay feels sticky between your fingers when moist and forms a ball that will not break apart when compressed in your hand. A great deal of organic matter and sand will need to be added annually to break down this soil's composition. Peat moss, compost, manure, and leaf mold plus sand will need to be added to the soil.

pH Levels

The majority of plants grow best in the neutral range of the pH scale which ranges from 0 to 14 with 7 being neutral. Some plants prefer alkaline soil with a pH over 8 and others enjoy an acidic soil with a pH under 6. Most plants will only grow well in their preferred pH soil. Acidic soil will occur under ever-

Butchart Gardens, Central Saanich BC

Respectfully Tend the Earth

Milner Gardens and Woodland, Qualicum Beach BC

Chapter Two

green trees and alkaline soils will be found close to the concrete of home foundations or where there was previously a concrete pad. Your soil's pH may also be high or low due to other reasons which may not be readily apparent. Choosing plants that thrive in your soil's natural pH level is the simplest option for a gardener, but sometimes you will prefer to alter the soil's pH in favor of a broader range of plant choice. A pH kit can be purchased from local nurseries for you to test how acidic or alkaline your soil is. When choosing to alter your soil's pH it is wise to have soil samples from several areas of your garden professionally tested. While a home test will give you an idea of what your soil's pH is, a professional test will be able to provide you with the exact pH count.

Acidic soil will become more neutral when dolomitic limestone is added to the soil. Alkaline soils will have their pH lowered when sulfur and aluminum or iron sulfates are added. It is important to seek professional advice prior to changing your soil's pH since too much of either substance can change your pH too drastically. The amount of amendment necessary will also depend on the presence of other nutrients in the soil. You can slowly lower your soil's pH by adding compost, peat, and lots of evergreen needles. It is

especially helpful to lower the pH level in a very small area when you wish to plant just one Azalea *(Rhododendron)* or other acid-loving plant. Adding pine needles to the soil before planting, adding a handful or two into the planting hole, and adding a top dressing of a couple of inches of needles will help adjust the pH in just the location of the plant. A top dressing of evergreen needles will be a necessary addition each spring. Some plants will change the color of their blossoms if the soil's pH is lowered just slightly under neutral. A pink hydrangea *(Hydrangea macrophylla)* will become

blue with a lower pH and just a handful of needles annually will help the hydrangea retain its blue flowers.

Chemical Versus Organic Assistance

When God commissioned Adam to care for the earth, he did not give him a wheelbarrow full of chemicals. After Adam and Eve sinned and were banished from the Garden of Eden, they were told thorns and briars would grow alongside their plants. Even then they were not given a basket full of chemical concoctions. Instead they pulled weeds

The Governors House Gardens, Victoria BC

Glacier Gardens, Juneau AK

by hand, made tools to ease their work and used animal power to plow and plant. They observed the natural order of plants and creatures and learned to use this order to their gardening advantage.

Fertilizing

Plants continually use up the available nutrients in the soil. For that reason it is important to add fertilizer each year, preferably in the spring when the plants begin a new burst of growth. Many gardeners rely on chemical fertilizers in order to quickly and conveniently give their plants a boost. There are however, many disadvantages to using this method. Chemical fertilizers can easily burn tender plants if not mixed or applied correctly. Chemicals will also deplete more quickly in hot weather when waterings are more frequent than in cooler weather. For this reason, you cannot apply the same amount of fertilizer at the same frequency during the whole garden season. It is also inadvisable to fertilize in extreme heat conditions. With hot temperatures, the plant will have an increased need for water. It will absorb too much of the fertilizer along with the water, again causing burning of the plant. Chemical fertilizers eventually become ineffective in soils that have not had their structure improved on a regular basis.

Organic fertilizers release their nutrients at a slower rate and with lesser concentrations making them safer to use with no risk of burning the plants by over applications. The only real instance of plant burn due to organic fertilization is when an overabundance of fresh manure has been used. It is essential to compost manures for a minimum of one year prior to applying on the garden. Composting will also kill any weed seeds that may exist in your manure. Once composted it is safe to use without risk of burning.

soluble fertilizer is the easiest to apply. Again, forego the many chemical fertilizers on the market targeted especially for container plants in favor of organic fertilizers. You will find organic water soluble fertilizers at most nurseries and garden centers or in mail order catalogues. Fertilizers made from

the water, which can then be safely used on your container plants. Add additional water after each use and dispose after about 8 weeks when all of the nutrients will have been leached from the manure or compost. The manure or compost can then be worked into the garden. Even though there are few nutrients remaining in the compost or manure, it will still improve the structural composition of the soil.

Preparing a New Garden

Deciding on what method to use in order to rid the soil of sod or weeds in preparation for a new garden will depend on how large the area is and how quickly you would like to begin gardening. It is unnecessary to use chemicals for preparation regardless of your time frame or the dimensions of your new garden.

Butchart Gardens, Central Saanich BC

Potted plants and hanging baskets have special nutrient requirements. Since the plant is in a small amount of soil it will usually require daily watering. As a result the nutrients in the soil will leach out fairly quickly. Planters and baskets need frequent fertilizer applications and a water

seaweed, fish oils, etc. are natural and friendly to the environment. Homemade liquid fertilizers, or compost tea, are also easily made. Place a burlap bag of manure or compost into a barrel filled with water and let it sit for at least 2 weeks. The nutrients will leach into

If you wish to remove sod quickly and efficiently, the best method is to rent a sod cutter from your local rental store. The added benefit of cutting the sod away from the new planting bed is that the sod can then be used to fill in any patchy areas of lawn you may have. A sod cutter is manageable enough for most anyone to use and can cut a tremendous amount of sod in a short period of time.

If you have time on your hands, there are a couple of sod and weed removal methods that will work well for you. In a reasonably sized garden, mark out your dimensions and cover the area with plastic, being sure to anchor the edges with stakes or weights. The sod and weeds will be cooked by the sun's heat trapped under the plastic. In the heat of the summer the area will be free of vegetation in just a few days. When the temperature is cool, it may take a couple of weeks. Even weed seeds will be killed due to the high temperatures reached beneath the plastic. Layering over the garden area takes longer to kill the sod and weeds, but in the end you have also added materials that add nutrients and structure to your soil.

To layer a new garden area, place 4-6 layers of newsprint over the garden. Then apply in any order a minimum of 3 inches total of manure, compost, good topsoil and vegetation such as grass clippings, shredded leaves, and kitchen scraps. The layers will smother the growing vegetation below. After a minimum of 6 weeks you can till the area, working the layers in through the soil. This is an especially good method to use during fall cleanup in preparation for a new spring garden. Fallen leaves, perennials, and annuals that have been cut back can be shredded and placed in the layers.

After the sod and weeds have been removed from your new garden bed, it is important to add compost, manure, and peat moss to build your soil. The amounts required will vary depending on your soil type, but a general rule of thumb would be 2 inches over the soil's surface prior to tilling in. Gardeners who invest the time and money to create great topsoil will grow the tallest plants with the largest blossoms in the neighborhood.

If you are planning to use landscape fabric with a mulch of wood chips, or stone in a bed containing mostly trees, shrubs, and grasses, it is even more imperative that you begin with good soil. Once the fabric and mulch is on top, you will not be improving the soil below again. Additional humus is recommended in this application. Mulched areas can be fertilized in future years with compost tea or organic liquid fertilizers.

Weed Control

Keeping weeds at bay is a continual job in the garden. Instead of relying on chemical weed killers, which are easily over sprayed or may drift with the wind and damage desirable plants, choose natural methods. Weeds are best managed before they emerge or when very small. A daily walk around the garden, pulling the odd weed as it is found, is far preferable to weeding extensively after a

couple of weeks. If the soil's surface is cultivated even once a week, weed seeds and emerging weeds will be exposed to the sun and wind and will not be able to root. When a garden is left to its own for even a couple of weeks, many weeds may have taken root and will at this point need to be pulled out by hand, a far more time consuming job than a quick weekly cultivation.

Weeds are happy to grow almost anywhere, in almost any soil type. Some weeds are so tenacious that they can spring through narrow cracks in interlock brick, flagstone patios and the tiniest cracks in concrete. It is difficult to remove such weeds since pulling them removes the top portion, but leaves the root intact to spring forth once again. There are some weeds that if pulled will actually increase production, budding forth from every sliver of root left in the soil. In order to eliminate these weeds, you will need to pour boiling water or spray an organic weed killer between the cracks. Use of these liquids will kill the root as well as the visible portion of the weed.

Mulches are a good way to deter weeds. Mulch is really any material that covers the soil. Various small stones and shredded or chipped bark are appropriate mulches over tree,

Butchart Gardens, Central Saanich BC

Respectfully Tend the Earth

shrub, and ornamental grass beds. They should be applied to a depth of three to four inches before settling. Perennials need more frequent applications of humus and should not be permanently mulched. An inch or two of grass clippings, shredded leaves, or finely shredded bark on perennial beds will help to keep weeds at bay. It is important to keep the clippings from touching the base of the plant so that the air is free to move around the plant's stem. As the material decomposes, it can just be worked into the soil. When choosing a mulch, cost will be a factor as well as the look you would like to achieve with your mulch. For areas where aesthetically pleasing mulches are not necessary, such as a vegetable garden, wet newsprint, pegged down landscape fabric, a thick layer of fallen leaves, or clean straw is sufficient. Around your home, where appearance is more important, other mulch material may be suitable. Stone mulch should complement your home's colors. Natural colored wood mulch is preferable to many of the artificial-looking dyed mulches. Wood chips that are too large do not settle well together and are easily blown out of place by the wind. It is better to choose relatively fine-shredded mulch that knits itself together as it settles. Coco shells or other light mulches do not usually stay in place very long. Although they are attractive, lightweight, and easy to work with, they blow about with the wind and you will spend too much time sweeping them from your path.

Pest Control

Insects are a part of each garden. Some are admired for their beauty, such as butterflies and ladybugs, or their unique character, like stick bugs. But it often seems that there are more insects which cause harm than are to be admired. There is nothing like taking pride in a perfect rose, only to look a little further down the stem to find a big chomp out of a rose petal. Insects are one of the more challenging things to manage in our gardens without resorting to chemical cures.

The best defense against damaging insects is a well-planned offense. Plants that are well cared for, have adequate water and fertilizer, and have been spaced and pruned to

38

allow for good air circulation will be far less likely to suffer the ill effects of damaging insects. Insects prey first on plants that are weak and in distress. Regular strolls through your garden will alert you to insect problems before they become unmanageable. A quick clip with garden pruners will remove a tent caterpillar nest before they have a chance to grow and begin to spread through your tree or plant. Dispose of it by burning the twig with the nest on it. Slug damage on low foliage plants can be kept to a minimum by regularly placing low containers of beer underneath the foliage. The slugs will be attracted to the scent of the yeast and will drown once in the container. At the first sign of earwigs, place small sections of 2-inch pipe under the affected plants. The earwigs will hide inside after they have feasted for the night. Each morning tap the pipe onto the side of a pail of soapy water. The earwigs will fall out of the pipe and be killed in the water. Hybrid tea, grandiflora, and floribunda roses are well known for their attraction of aphids. If aphids appear on your roses, pour soapy water over the rose. Soapy water will need to be applied every couple of days until there is no longer any sign of aphids. Reusing your dishwater is ideal for this purpose. There are also many roses that are not nearly as susceptible to

aphids as these varieties. Plant shrub roses *(Rosa rugosa)* varieties and enjoy the rose without the hassle. Large insects such as potato bugs can be hand picked.

Beneficial insects such as ladybugs, lacewings, and predator wasps are available through mail order catalogues. They can be placed about your garden with the intention of the beneficial insect devouring the damaging bugs. While this is very helpful in an indoor environment such as a conservatory, the reality is that the beneficial insects you purchased will be just as likely to fly off and consume your neighbors' bad bugs as they will yours. These beneficial insects are therefore not of great value for your backyard garden.

Organic insect sprays and powders work well to eradicate bad insects, however many also kill beneficial insects. While they are preferable to chemical sprays, it is better to use no insecticide at all. If you develop healthy plants and you are willing to take a daily walk through your garden, you will be alerted to problem insects before they have a chance to do any real damage. Finally, keep in mind that all of God's plants and creatures need to coexist together for a natural balance in our gardens. We therefore ought to develop a more realistic sense of what the "perfect" garden looks like and accept that from time to time, we will have foliage with minor insect damage.

Watering

Gardens that receive regular water have plants that are strong, healthy, and less susceptible to damaging insects or diseases. Even gardens planted primarily with drought tolerant species will need additional water in particularly long periods of hot, dry weather. Drought tolerant plants also need to begin their life in your garden with sufficient water in order to establish strong roots. Once established, they will withstand periods of low water. When rain isn't falling on our gardens as frequently or sufficiently as we would like, we will need to get out the hoses or turn on the irrigation system to satisfy our plants' thirst. When this is necessary, it is important to choose the watering method that will make the most efficient use of water. The abundance of fresh water we have been accustomed to can no longer be taken for granted. It is important to be mindful of our water consumption, as we now know that it is not a limitless resource.

Water Collection

It is amazing how much water can be collected, just by using rain barrels. Rain barrels located under the eaves of our home will collect all of the rain that falls on our roofs. Rain barrels should have a lid since standing water is a breeding ground for mosquito larvae. A flow valve located near the bottom of the barrel will make it easy to access the water. Organic fertilizer can be added directly to the rain barrel so that we are always adding nutrients to our plants as we water.

Irrigation

The most efficient way to water is by automatic irrigation, preferably irrigation that is drip fed through lines directly onto the ground. Irrigation systems should be set up to run in the very early morning hours before the sun rises. This way almost 100 percent of the water is used by the plants. While not everyone can afford the luxury of an irrigation system, it does save on water use and can lower your water bill if you are on a metered system. It is important to include a rain gauge in your irrigation system. It is usually priced as an extra by irrigation companies, but should, ideally, be standard on all systems. A rain gauge will measure the quantity of rain that falls and will override the system's automation so that it will not run for a period of time after it rains.

Overhead Sprinklers

Using portable, overhead sprinklers wastes the most water of any watering system. Sprinklers are frequently left on much longer than intended. Well meaning gardeners turn on the sprinkler, become distracted, and forget to move it or turn it off. Sprinklers are generally used when the sun is out. The sun will evaporate much of the water before it hits the ground for which it was intended. Sprinklers are sometimes accidentally left running all night long. Plants dislike cool, wet foliage and mildew diseases flourish in the garden that is sprinkled regularly at night. If sprinkling is your method of watering, buy a sprinkler with a built-in timer or add a timer to your hose connection. The timer will turn

Danielle Burgsma

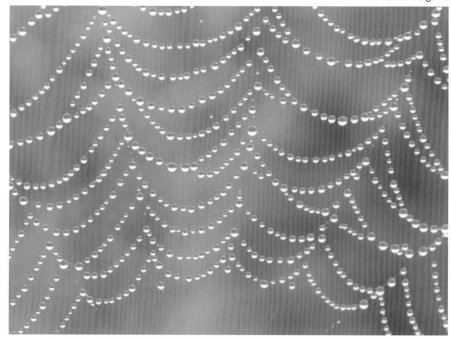

the sprinkler off automatically so that you are free to run your errands.

Soaker Hoses

Soaker hoses make very efficient use of water. Hoses with tiny holes all along its length are laid directly onto gardens. The water disperses slowly and waters only the ground around the plants. It is important to add a timer to your hose connection so that the water will not be running for longer than necessary. When using a soaker hose, the time you leave the water running is much shorter than when using a sprinkler since very little of the water is being lost to the air, but is directed wholly to the plants' root systems. Since no water is resting on the foliage, plants are less likely to get diseases such as mildew.

There Is No Waste in a Garden

God designed the plant cycle so that no part of any plant is wasted. Fallen foliage, spent blossoms, and broken twigs all become food for the very plant it came from. Insects and worms break down the debris and return their own waste to enrich your soil. Examine the earth below the canopy of a hardwood forest. Feel the richness of the soil in your hands and smell the scent of the woods.

Hatley Park National Historic Site, Victoria BC

Respectfully Tend the Earth

side of your garden beds, mow over the debris three or four times, and then blow the finely chopped materials back onto the gardens. By the time spring arrives, the debris will have mostly decomposed leaving food that will attract earthworms and feed your flowers. The real bonus of this cleanup method is there is no back breaking pulling, shoveling, and raking going on in your garden. You will be sitting on your deck sipping hot chocolate while your neighbors slave behind their rakes, shovels, and hedge clippers. They'll be peeking over the fence in wonder at how you were able to clean up your fall gardens so quickly.

There are instances when you should not use fallen leaves as food for your gardens. Black Walnut *(Juglans nigra)* and Oak *(Quercus)* leaves should be composted for a minimum of six months prior to using on your garden. The Black Walnut foliage needs to compost well to eradicate the chemical juglone so it doesn't harm your plants. Oak leaves should be used only in areas where acidic soil is welcome. Rose leaves should be removed and burned rather than being reused on the garden. Typical rose problems can remain in the foliage and infect the soil, causing problems for the rose again the next growing season if the leaves are worked into the soil below the roses.

This is the type of garden soil you are seeking. I almost weep when I drive through towns and see bags and bags of leaves set out for city pick up. All of those leaves should have been used to feed their own gardens. Instead, people are relying on chemical fertilizers at a financial cost to themselves and an environmental cost to the earth. A free supply of organic fertilizer is available in each and every garden. Making use of the free fertilizer is quick and

simple and is less back breaking than raking and bagging leaves. Instead of raking your leaves, mow them into windrows and then mow over them several times until they are finely chopped. Spread the resulting materials over your gardens.

When putting your gardens to rest for the winter, set your lawn mower at its tallest setting and mow over all of the perennials and annuals in your beds. Blow the plant material out-

The Perfect Lawn

Many homeowners take great pride in their perfect, thick, green grass void of any semblance of weeds. Achieving this sort of lawn is near impossible without the heavy, regular use of chemicals. The quest for the perfect lawn has created the largest use of chemicals within the horticultural industry. Instead of saturating our ground water systems with these unnecessary chemicals, we should reevaluate what a perfect lawn is. In my opinion, a perfect lawn is one that stays green most of the season. It is a lawn planted with a variety of drought tolerant grasses and some plants that others consider weeds, such as yarrow and clover. Yarrow *(Achillea millefolium)* is a very drought tolerant plant with fine foliage that blends in very well with grass mixtures. The yarrow will remain green in the toughest drought and as an added bonus it is a natural mosquito repellant.

In a small lawn, weeds such as thistle and dandelion can be managed by hand. In a large lawn, spot spray large weeds with an organic based weed killer. Or, embrace the wildflowers that may inhabit your lawn, harvest those dandelion leaves for your salads, and turn the flower petals into dandelion wine.

Regular watering will keep your lawn green and thick, but lawns do not need nearly as much water as most people think. Use a rain gauge to measure the quantity of water sprinkled on your lawn. One inch of water per week is enough to grow a healthy green lawn. Less water is required if your lawn was planted with drought tolerant grass varieties. It is important to water your lawn deeply, rather than several shallow waterings. Shallow waterings only encourage the roots to stay near the top of the soil whereas deep waterings will encourage the roots to dive deeper into the soil. Shallow rooted lawns will be less able to withstand drought conditions. Mowing your lawn too short will also create shallow roots. Longer grass will grow deeper roots and therefore healthier grass.

Over a period of time, thatch can smother a healthy lawn. The resulting compacted soil under the grass will prevent good air circulation and water penetration to the roots. Thatch is an accumulation of dead grass and debris which needs to be combed off of the lawn. De-thatch your lawn when excessive clippings begin to accumulate. A thatch layer that is over half an inch thick can also harbor insects, which may be harmful to your lawn. Raking or using a de-thatching machine will work equally well in eliminating your thatch layer. De-thatching and aerating your lawn will help to improve the air circulation and water penetration in your lawn. Maintaining your lawn in this manner without the use of chemicals will produce a very healthy, thick, green grass that weeds will not be able to seed into.

Lawn Alternatives

Use alternatives for grass on slopes and areas where there is little foot traffic. There is a large selection of ground cover plants for both full sun and full shade conditions. Most ground covers are invasive by nature and a few plants can blanket a large area in a very small amount of time. Plants placed at a rate of one four inch plant per two square feet will spread and cover the area in one year. If budget is an issue, one plant per three square feet will fill in the area within two years.

It is essential to care for newly planted areas regularly until the ground cover fills in. Prepare the ground well to eliminate any existing weeds and weed seeds. Mulching the area with two inches of shredded bark mulch will greatly diminish weeding and watering needs while the new plants become established. It is important to remove weeds regularly until the ground cover fills in. Once established, the ground cover will reward the gardener with an almost maintenance free area in future years. Ground covers can provide all-season foliage color, carpets of floral displays, and wafts of scent to perfume your garden. A large majority of ground covers are very drought tolerant once established and are resistant to many insect and disease problems.

If the area you desire to plant ground cover is an area that receives some foot traffic, you will need to lay a few flagstones to create a path or you will need to limit your choice to steppable plants. Plants such as Thymes *(Thymus)*, and Moss *(Sagina)*, can take a considerable amount of foot traffic and are very appropriate for well-traveled paths. If you are covering a slope, your options are much more varied. You do not need to choose low growing plants alone. Daylily *(Hemerocallis)*, and Hosta *(Hosta)*, are quick covering plants that require very little future maintenance.

Gardening, part of tending God's earth, is an amazing interaction between humans and the rest of creation. If we are willing to put more thought into our plant choices, concentrate on good nutrition, hydration, and regular, consistent maintenance; if we have a willingness to accept almost perfect, rather than strive for absolute perfect plants and lawns, we will be on our way to chemical-free home gardens. And, we'll be working in harmony with God's natural design for ecosystems.

Butchart Gardens, Central Saanich BC

Deadnettle (*Lamium maculatum*), Goutweed (*Aegopodium podagraria* 'Variegatum'), Lily of the Valley (*Convallaria majalis*)

Myrtle (*Vinca minor*), Sweet Woodruff (*gallium odoratum*), Bearberry (*cotoneaster*)

Thyme (*Thymus serpyllum*), Stonecrop (*Sedum acre*), Spurge (*Euphorbia procumbens*)

Respectfully Tend the Earth

HONOR TREES

"You will live in joy and peace.

The mountains and the hills will burst into song,

and the trees of the field will clap their hands!"

Isaiah 55:12 NLT

Butchart Gardens, Central Saanich BC

It is amazing to see how God created the earth. In the beginning, every living thing, whether plant, animal, or human, was perfect and lived in perfect harmony with each other. *"God looked over all he had made, and he saw that it was excellent in every way," Genesis 1:31 NLT.* God created living things to interact and benefit from others. In the plant world, one obvious display of God's plan of interdependence is his creation of trees. Trees are essential for the very air we breathe, for our comfortable shelters, and much of the food that we eat.

God gave Adam and Eve, and all of humankind, the great gift and responsibility of looking after his creation. Unfortunately, humankind's disobedience changed everything. Instead of valuing and tending our trees and forests, we've destroyed many of them due to lack of foresight, or in the name of "progress." We need to acknowledge our folly, take up the spade, and plant trees in our urban spaces, along our roadsides, and in decimated forests.

Author's Garden, Goderich ON

Role of Trees

Choosing to include trees within your landscape has far more significance than aesthetics alone. Trees are the earth's primary air cleansers and coolers. Trees clean our air by breathing in carbon dioxide and breathing out oxygen. The cooling effects that tree canopies have on our earth should not be underestimated. Trees shade the earth's floor and waters from the sun thus helping to keep the earth's temperature in check. Continual decreases in the earth's forests and increased use of fossil fuels have con-

tributed to global warming. Planting additional trees in our gardens and urban spaces as well as reforesting what we have lost will help to combat the negative impact that carbon dioxide has on our atmosphere.

Trees also help to manage the amount of erosion which occurs on farmers' fields and along steep banks. Trees planted as windrows between fields will lessen the wind's strength and its effect on the first few inches of topsoil. The loss of valuable topsoil is considerably reduced as a result of well-placed trees. The

roots of trees serve to stabilize steep banks. It is important to preserve trees along banks, particularly if they are located next to a body of water where winds harshly whip up the bank and water lashes at its base causing irreversible erosion. Many home and cottage owners along lakes and oceans cut down trees or remove a significant amount of lower limbs so they may have a better view of the water. When too many lower limbs are removed, a tree may become top heavy and be more susceptible to blowing down in the wind. When shoreline trees are

Hatley Park National Historic Site, Victoria BC

Honor Trees

removed or blown over, the bank is left without the web of roots that was necessary to keep it stable. It is important to replace any fallen or removed trees with new trees and quick-growing shrubbery as soon as possible to keep the bank stable.

Energy Conservation Benefits

Thoughtfully placed trees in a garden can reduce costs related to heating and cooling your home. Mature deciduous trees planted on southern and western exposures close to your home benefit two ways. In the summer the shade provided by the trees' foliage will prevent the sun from penetrating through your windows, thus reducing the need for air conditioning. As fall approaches, leaves fall to the ground and sun can shine through the trees' branches allowing in sunlight to warm your home during the cold months of the year. Placing evergreen trees in the path of prevailing winds will help reduce heating costs in winter. Planting tall hedges or collections of tall evergreens on the boundaries of your garden will cut the force of the wind and cold before it reaches your home. It is important to plant the trees far enough away from your home so that when mature, they will not shade the house when the sun is at its lowest point of the horizon.

Practical Landscape Benefits

Planting a shade tree adjacent to a patio, or placing a bench under a large shade tree for a private getaway will offer us a cool area to sit and relax in the heat of the summer. Placing children's play equipment

MacNaughton Park, Exeter ON

under the shade of a mature deciduous tree will give them a cool place to play and keep them out of the harmful rays of the sun.

In an urban garden, we have no con-trol over the view to our neighbor's yard or the streetscape beyond our property boundaries. Evergreen trees will hide undesirable views in all seasons. Evergreen trees will also help to muffle street noises, and sounds created by neighbors enjoying their own gardens. Trees can provide privacy. While evergreen trees will shield us all year long, deciduous trees are often sufficient to provide privacy, as they are in leaf at the times we will be outside in our gardens. Evergreen hedges make a

Honor Trees

Niagra Parks, Niagra Falls ON

wonderful living alternative to wood, chain link, or composite fencing. Good, low maintenance choices would include tall varieties of Cedar *(Thuja)*, Yew *(Taxus)*, and Juniper *(Juniperus)*.

Trees can provide a welcoming entrance to our home. A long laneway flanked on each side by mature Maples *(Acer platanoides)*, or a shorter laneway with Magnolias *(Magnolia)*, will give a sense of entry. It is important to remember in areas that receive snowfall to only plant deciduous trees on either side of a laneway. Evergreens will only serve to trap fallen snow on our laneway, causing us to spend too much time and energy on snow removal. Deciduous trees on the other hand, allow wind to blow through the trunks and branches, thus sending the snow over the laneway instead of settling upon it. A long laneway with tall evergreens on either side also tends to feel slightly claustrophobic. The best arrangement of trees alongside driveways is one that uses the same tree species throughout. Simplicity far outweighs variety in this case. Trees of different species or trees that alternate from deciduous to coniferous become distracting to the eye.

If your property offers a beautiful vista it can be accentuated if it is framed. Using trees on either side of a preferred view gives focus to the area. A small garden can use columnar trees to frame a view without taking up too much space. A large variety of conifers and deciduous trees have been bred to be very narrow in size. When choosing narrow trees, look for trees which include the word *columnare* or *fastigiata* behind their species name. A favorite columnar tree is the Pyramid Oak *(Quercus robur fastigiata),* or an even narrower version, *Quercus robur fastigiata* 'Crimson Spire'. The oak leaves will persist well into the winter, making it desirable in the winter as well as the summer. A large garden can frame a view with a collection of trees on either side. In the larger garden, the trees do not have to be the same variety as long as they present similar weight to both sides of the view. Each assortment of trees should take up a similar amount of space.

Right Tree, Right Place

When choosing trees for our home gardens, it is important to consider what size the tree will be at maturity. The single biggest mistake most people make when they plant trees is to plant them too close together, or too close to driveways, sidewalks, and buildings. When picking out a young tree in a seven gallon pot at a nursery, it is hard to imagine how large it will actually become. Many trees are cut

Butchart Gardens, Central Saanich BC

Honor Trees

53

Horse Chestnut (*Aesculus hippocastanum*), Catalpa (*Catalpa speciosa*), Purple Robe Locust (*Robinia pseudoacacia*)
Cedar (*Thuja occidentalis* 'Smargd'), Korean Spruce (*Abies koreana* 'Silberlocke'), Austrian Pine (*Pinus nigra*)
Redbud (*Cercis Canadensis*), Japanese Maple (*Acer plantinoides*), Saucer Magnolia (*Magnolia grandiflora*)

down at the prime of their life because they were improperly placed. Take the time to find out how large their spread will eventually be and space the tree with that as your guide.

Scale and proportion are important to note before choosing a tree for your garden. A tree needs to be in the proper size relationship with the house it is planted beside. A small bungalow would look terribly small and out of scale if a seventy foot Colorado Blue Spruce *(Picea pungens glauca* 'Coloradus') was planted in front of it. The same tree would look very appropriate planted beside a two- or three-story home. The size relationship would fit. A better tree to be planted in front of the bungalow would be a smaller cultivar of Colorado Blue Spruce such as *Picea pungens glauca* 'Fat Albert'.

Messy trees, which continually loose small foliage and twigs, drop pollen, petals, or fruit, ought not to be planted too close to the house, driveway, or sidewalk. Trees such as willows are best left for large, open expanses as they loose pollen and leaves from early spring into December. In addition, any wind that blows will take with it twigs and small branches that will need to be raked up. Crab apple trees situated too close to a walkway may leave stains underfoot from fallen apples. These fallen treats will

55

Honor Trees

need to be continually swept from walkways so that they will not be tracked into the house.

When we plant a new tree, we not only need to look around; we need to look up as well. Trees which will grow taller than overhead wires will become a hazard during wind and ice storms. These trees will also need to be pruned regularly so there is clearance between the branches and the wire. A tree pruned to accommodate wires becomes lopsided looking and unattractive. It is better to choose a variety that will not grow above the lowest wire when mature. There are many smaller, attractive trees available.

In rural areas where we rely on septic beds for sanitation, we need to be aware of the perimeter of the weeping bed. No trees or shrubs should be planted within or too close to this perimeter as damage will eventually occur to the weeping bed. Roots will find their way to this fertile ground and will entwine around the pipes and fill drainage holes, thus clogging the system. Costly repairs will result. Gardens placed near or on top of septic beds may be planted with perennials, annuals and grasses.

Black Walnut trees *(Juglans nigra)*

produce a root inhibiting chemical called juglone which affects a wide variety of plants' vigor and growth. A mature black walnut can have a root circumference over sixty feet. Many plants will not grow within this juglone affected area. Juglone can contaminate the soil for up to a year after a tree has been removed. Since the area affected can be so large, it is important to look over the fence to the neighbor's yard as well as your own. If there is a black walnut tree in the vicinity of your garden, choose to place only those plants that will be unaffected by juglone. It is good to note as well, that black walnut trees and Red Maples *(Acer rubrum),* should not be planted near horses' paddocks as they are toxic to horses and ponies. It is inadvisable to use fresh leaves and woodchips from black walnut trees as mulch or compost on your garden. They are, however, safe to use after composting for six months.

Salt is also a hindrance to the healthy growth of trees. Trees located alongside roads or sidewalks that use salt to melt winter's snow are at risk of damage caused by windborne salt spray and saline soils resulting from runoff. Some trees that are located near the seaside will also display poor health due to salt spray from the sea. Damage is seen especially in spring when leaf buds fail or are

Butchart Gardens, Central Saanich BC

distorted. Twigs die back and evergreen needles begin to brown from the tip inwards. Young trees are more susceptible than established trees. Trees may be protected from salt spray with a burlap wrap or snow fencing, but roots will still be affected if there is sufficient salt runoff collected near the roots. To help reduce the negative effect of salt-saturated soils, water soil deeply as soon as the ground thaws to flush the salt out of the soil.

Evergreen and oak trees cause the soil below them to become acidic. If you walk through a pine or cedar forest, you will notice that the ground is covered with a layer of shed needles or foliage but there is almost nothing green growing on the forest floor. This is due to the acidity of the soil and the fact that it takes a considerable amount of time to break down coniferous needles. They create a thick carpet in which seeds cannot see their way through to germinate. If you wish to garden below these trees, it is important to choose plants that thrive in acidic soil conditions. Gardens placed under acidic trees will also require a generous helping of compost or manure and additional water as the tree roots will be the first to gulp down any water that becomes available.

How wonderful it would be if each person planted one tree on Arbor Day. Just one tree; somewhere, someplace. It might be in their backyard, in an urban public space or perhaps in a wilderness area needing reforestation. What a marvelous living legacy we could leave for the generations yet to come!

DELIGHT IN SEASONS

"As long as the earth endures,

seedtime and harvest, cold and heat,

summer and winter, day and night will never cease."

Genesis 8:22 NIV

Author's Garden, Goderich ON

We are very blessed in most of North America to have markedly changing seasons. We are left ever anticipating the next change of scenery. Each season comes with its own unique beauty. Every season is enjoyed for different reasons: the crunch of snow under foot on a winter's day, gardens bursting to life in springtime, relaxing under the shade of an old oak on a hot summer's day, and watching the fall landscape turn into a kaleidoscope of colors.

Author's Garden, Goderich ON

Winter Gardens

Winter gardens can be magical places where snow layers on evergreen boughs, frost kisses individual stems of ornamental grasses and icicles dangle from twisted branches. Winter is the time to walk in your garden and assess its true value in what we often consider the bleakest months. Evergreens, branches from deciduous trees and shrubs, pergolas, gazebos, and garden art such as statues and urns provide the shapes and structures or 'bones' of the garden when foliage and flowers are absent. A garden with great 'bones' will be a garden that shines in winter as well as during the bountiful, blooming summer season.

A truly great winter garden is attained by purposeful planning and attention to detail. Including conifers, grasses, and interestingly branched trees and shrubs will increase the value of the planted portions of your garden. Attention to the inclusion and placement of garden art and built structures will provide lasting interest after the last leaf has fallen.

It is important to consider the garden view from inside your home since we will be looking at our gardens primarily through our windows rather than from our patios.

Built Form

Built form refers to structures such as fences, gates, arbors, pergolas, gazebos, and walls from nearby buildings. The material and shapes of these structures are left bare when perennials have been cut back, shrubs have lost their foliage and vines are but clinging skeletons. Built form can be a permanent and costly part of your garden, therefore its placement and material should be carefully considered.

Pergolas and fences must not block an important view, but rather, should frame it. Place tall stakes in the ground prior to building such structures. Look through the stakes from several angles to be sure their place-

MacNaughton Park, Exeter ON

ment takes advantage of the most attractive view beyond. The garden gate ought to be positioned for traffic flow, but also think about the vista when the gate is open.

In urban areas, we do not have control over the borrowed view from our neighbor's walls. If a neighbor's unsightly structures are visible, a well placed structure in our own garden can help to mask its negative impact.

Garden Art

Garden art is any accent which enhances the overall look of a garden but is not plant material or built structure. Statues, urns, obelisks, and benches may be the first thing that comes to mind when we think about garden art, but driftwood, rockery, bird houses, wagon wheels, and cedar posts are also art when well positioned. There is garden art to suit anyone's budget, from high end marble to more modest concrete statuary and custom wrought iron benches to handmade twig furniture. With such a large range of budget, no garden should be without an artistic element.

Choice of garden art is a matter of personal taste, but its placement is critical to create punctuation marks and balance within the garden. The art must be in scale with its surroundings, be secondary to the plantings and be used in moderation. Too much art is dis-

61

Delight in Seasons

tracting to the eye and takes away from the natural beauty of the garden itself. Well chosen and carefully placed art can create focal points or subtle accents within the garden.

Urns and planters overflow with cascading flowers in summer, but be sure to use them in your winter garden as well. Don't be tempted to throw out your hanging baskets after the blossoms have succumbed to frost. Rather, fill them with evergreen boughs, red or yellow twig Dogwood *(Cornus alba* 'Sibirica*')* *(Cornus stolonifera* 'Flaviramea*'),* dried grasses, curly branches and dried hydrangea flowers.

Plant Form

Plant form is the structure of a shrub or tree when no foliage is present, perennial plants which maintain form by foliage drying back, and evergreens that contribute both foliage and branch structure through all seasons. The first category which comes to mind in a winter garden is conifers. While conifers are admittedly king of the garden in winter, grasses, deciduous trees and shrubs add interest as well. Each of these types of plants contributes unique qualities. A well planted winter garden will include all of these plants in combination.

In many areas, snow does not cover the ground throughout the entire winter; in some areas it barely leaves a dusting upon the ground. In winter, turf is brown or a mix of green and brown and does not offer any attraction for the garden. For this reason it is essential to include plantings for the ground plane in a winter garden. Including ground cover plantings in large areas or in pockets here and there, provide carpets of color all year long. Great winter ground covers include Periwinkle *(Vinca minor)*, Mondo Grass *(Ophiopogon planiscapus),* Carpet Sedum *(Sedum acre),* low growing Junipers *(Juniperus procumbens),* low growing Cotoneasters *(Cotoneaster dammeri),* as well as many others.

Conifers have come a long way in recent years and provide a large color palette all on their own. These are the plants which will give us color even during winter. Various shades of green, blue, and yellow conifers are available to include in our gardens. Conifers offer subtle color changes in the winter as well.

Beauty Berry (*Calllicarpa americana*), Bearberry (*Cotoneaster adpressus*), Porcelain Berry (*Brevipedunculata* 'Elegans')
Paperbark Maple (*Acer griseum*), Dawn Redwood (*Metasequoia glyptostroboides*), London Plane (*Platanus x acerifolia*)
Kerria (*Kerria japonica*), Red Twig Dogwood (*Cornus alba* 'Siberica'), Yellow Twig Dogwood (*Cornus stolonifera* 'Flaviramea')

63

Delight in Seasons

Some turn duller and darker, while others turn from their summer green to either bronze, gold, or burgundy. Bar Harbor Juniper *(Juniperus horizontalis* 'Bar Harbor*')* has grey-green foliage in summer which turns to a mauve-purple color in winter. Reingold Cedar *(Thuja occidentalis* 'Reingold*')* changes from a bright golden color to a deep copper-bronze. Using golden foliaged conifers as accents planted among green and blue conifers will create a more striking show than if they were to be planted en masse.

Use of conifers in all of their sizes and shapes will create winter interest in all levels of our garden. Tall Colorado Blue Spruce *(Picea pungens glauca)* or White Pine *(Pinus strobes)* will give us evergreen grandeur: medium conifers such as Cedar *(Thuja)* varieties will anchor our gardens: and smaller evergreens such as Yew *(Taxus)* and Boxwood *(Buxus)* will give us lower interest.

Topiaries, trees or shrubs that are trained or trimmed into interesting shapes, are a great addition to any garden. When created from evergreens, they remain attractive all year long. They may enhance a formal garden with clipped spirals and hedges or add whimsy when trimmed into animal shapes.

Winter Garden Schedule
Water evergreens in mild periods to prevent damage from desiccation
Clean and sharpen gardening tools
Order seeds and plants from catalogues
Start seeds in greenhouse or under grow lights in late winter
Read gardening books to increase your gardening knowledge and inspire new gardens come spring

Deciduous trees offer the winter garden interesting branch patterns and texture through peeling bark. Excellent choices for interesting bark are the London Plane Tree *(Platanus x hispanica)* offering bark reminiscent of camouflage army garments Striped Maple *(Acer pensylvanicum)* with markedly striped bark and Paper Birch *(Betula papyrifera)* with its bright white peeling bark. Textural trunks come from trees such as Paperbark Maple *(Acer griseum)* as well as a large variety of mature trees with thick, fissured bark. All trees add winter value through their branches but trees which are particularly twisted are of added sculptural interest. Old Mulberry trees *(Morus austalis* 'Unryu*')* and Corkscrew Willow *(Salix babylonica var. pekinesis* 'Tortuosa*')* boast very twisting branches and are more attractive in winter than in any other season.

Shrubs which are stripped of their leaves after the fall can offer remarkable color, attractive dried flowers and good branch structure. Red and yellow twigged Dogwood *(Cornus alba* 'Sibirica*'),(Cornus stolinifera* 'Flaviramea*')* show best without their foliage and add striking color against the white snow. Many shrubs produce vibrantly colored berries and rose hips that dot the landscape with bright red, orange and black. Other shrubs offer clusters of seed heads or

64

dried flowers. Hydrangea *(Hydrangea)* of any variety will hold their large, dried flower heads through winter's toughest storms to peek through drifts of snow. Witch Hazel *(Hamamelis)* varieties grace the garden with yellow or orange spidery flowers during winter.

Plants which dry back (as opposed to those which die back), though dormant in winter, retain their form and structure and hold their interest. Grasses are especially great winter dry back plants. They become straw colored or sometimes apricot colored, holding their fluffy plumes through the toughest winter winds. Some perennials also remain upright and offer clusters of attractive seed heads. Showy Sedum *(Sedum spectibile)*, Purple Cone Flower *(Echinacea)* and Black Eye Susan *(Rudbeckia)* are all good choices to leave standing for their off season displays.

A few plants will pop up from beneath the snow and provide a most welcome flower. Blossoms from Snowdrops *(Galanthus)*, Winter Aconites *(Eranthis)* and Christmas Rose *(Helleborus)* will greet us just as the snow begins to melt into spring.

It is also possible to bring the outside in during winter. Many spring blooming trees and shrubs can be forced to bloom long before their time. A few branches of Forsythia *(Forsythia)* can be cut in early January and burst forth with bright yellow blossoms just a couple of weeks later. Many fruit trees such as Magnolia *(Magnolia)* and Quince *(Chaenomeles)* are easily forced. Look for branches carrying lots of buds, cut them and place in a vase with lukewarm water. Place in a warm location inside your home and a week or two later they will break bud. Forcing branches in early January will take more time than branches forced in late March. Forsythia cut in late March may bloom

in as few as five days. Cutting branches a week or so apart will ensure a constant display of spring blossoms all winter long.

Winter also provides gardeners with well deserved rest. There is very little to do in winter to maintain your garden. Instead it's time to sit back, relax, and dream of the new soil to be turned come spring.

Spring Gardens

Spring is one of the most glorious seasons of all. Gardens once again become alive with color, birds come back to serenade and butterflies float by. Watching the transformation of what was bare or brown quickly transform into that which is green and alive is a most amazing gift. *"See! The winter is past; the rains are over and gone. Flowers appear on the earth; the season of singing has come, the cooing of doves is heard in our land." Song of Songs 2:11, 12 NIV*

Flowering trees are the glory of spring gardens, bursting forth with blossoms soon to be followed by fresh green foliage. Driveways lined with Crab Apple Trees *(Malus)*, gardens spotted with Magnolia *(Magnolia)*, Redbuds *(Cercis canadensis)*, Golden Chain Trees *(Laburnum)* and Weeping Cherries

65

(Prunus subhirtella pendula) make striking displays as the blossoms verily smother each and every branch. Hundreds of blossoms will mat the ground as fresh, new leaves replace the fading flowers. No other season will offer such tall and massive floral displays.

Under the trees' canopies and in pockets throughout our gardens spring bulbs pop up greeting us with soft pastels and vibrant reds and oranges. Hyacinths scent the air and raindrops renew lawns into fresh green carpets.

Since we are eager to see new life after a long winter, we should include the earliest blooming varieties of trees, shrubs and bulbs in our gardens. The spring garden season can be stretched by carefully choosing plant material that provides early, mid and late season blossoms. Forsythia *(Forsythia)*, Lilac *(Syringa)*, Beauty Bush *(Kolkwitzia)*, and Quince *(Chaenomeles)* all bloom at different times during spring.

Bulbs in the same family have several varieties which bloom a week or so apart for a long floral show. When planting Tulips *(Tulipa)*, for instance, plant several varieties to extend the blooming season for many weeks. The first tulips to bloom will be *Tulipa gesneriana 'Giuseppe Verdi'*, *Tulipa aucheriana* will carry on midseason, *Tulipa biflora 'Blue Parrot'* will provide late flowers and the last blossoms will be found on *Tulipa sprengeri*. A general rule of thumb is that greigii tulips bloom early in the season; fosteriana, triumph, and Kaufmania tulips bloom mid season; and lily, parrot, and double-flowered tulips bloom late in the season. Darwin tulip varieties will bloom at various times throughout the entire season. Fortunately most garden centre displays clearly mark if a tulip blooms early, mid or late season.

It is a good thing we have had all winter to rest from gardening since spring is a season when there is much work to be done. A bit of extra hard work in spring will help to minimize the work necessary through the summer season.

Author's Garden, Goderich ON

Author's Garden, Goderich ON

Delight in Seasons

Spring Garden Schedule		
APRIL	MAY	JUNE
Rake any leaves remaining from fall lawn and gardens and place in compost	Cultivate gardens to eliminate emerging weed seeds	Continue cultivating the soil on a weekly basis to prevent weed seeds from germinating or growing too large
De-thatch and aerate lawn; rake and add grass seed to any thin area	Provide support for plants such as peony before they are in full bloom	Braid daffodil foliage, fold over and tuck into itself to hide fading foliage
Cut back grasses and butterfly bushes	Plant annuals	Pull out other spring bulb foliage when well yellowed and 'ripe'
Prune any winter-damaged branches from trees and shrubs	Plant warm season vegetables (tomatoes, beans, etc.)	Remove spent blooms on lilacs to increase future blossom quantity and size
Uncover or untie any shrubs which were protected over winter; remove tree guards	Mow lawn at two to two and half inches	Prune flowering shrubs shortly after flowering
Amend soil with peat moss and manure or compost	Remove suckers from grafted trees as they appear	Prune evergreens
Divide perennials		
Mulch gardens		
Clean out small ponds and water features; re-install pumps		
Prepare vegetable garden, plant cold season vegetables (spinach, peas, etc.)		
Remove soil hills from roses		

Butchart Gardens, Central Saanich BC

68

Summer Gardens

Summer is the time to enjoy our gardens to the fullest. We stroll through paths abounding with colorful flowers and rest with a good book under the canopy of large shade trees. Our families gather on our patios for summer barbeques and our friends reminisce around our back yard campfires. A well planned garden will invite us to spend much more time out of doors than inside.

By the time July rolls around, perennials have spread their leaves and annuals have grown to fill up any vacant portions of our garden. If time was well spent in spring maintenance, gardens will need very little

attention during July and August. A well filled out garden will prevent many weeds from germinating due to the lack of sunlight that reaches the soil. Soil which is sufficiently shaded by foliage will also keep the soil moist for longer periods of time.

A well maintained garden will allow us to venture off on family camping trips and frequent outings to the beach or the neighborhood swimming pool. Keeping to a weekly maintenance schedule will minimize work. A quick run over the soil with a long handled hand cultivator, stirring up weed seeds before they germinate, is much quicker than hand weeding gardens when weeds have been allowed to take root over sev-

eral weeks. Watering as necessary is crucial to healthy plants, which will then be more able to withstand any damage from insects or diseases.

There are so many colorful blooming summer annuals, perennials and shrubs that it is hard to choose the ones to include in our gardens. Anyone with limited space can only choose a small selection from the vast bloomers available. When planting bloomers in limited spaces, opt for colors that work well together. Choose perennials and shrubs with the longest bloom period. Hydrangea *(Hydrangea)* is a sure pleaser because it typically begins blooming in July and continues on till frost softens its colors. New varieties are being introduced that begin blooming earlier and continue to set new flowers throughout the season. Perennials with short flowering periods should be used in mod-

Abkhazi Gardens, Victoria BC

eration and need to have really great foliage to sustain their garden value. A Shasta daisy *(Chrysanthemum maximum* 'Alaska'*)* is a garden favorite for its abundant daisy flowers, but has very little value when the flowers have faded. Its stems tend to flop over and the foliage becomes leggy after flowering. It would be best kept for the larger garden where foliage plants can be planted in front to mask the plant after it blooms. Larger gardens can have many garden areas with different color themes in each area. Larger gardens also have the benefit of layering plants more effectively to allow for a continual show of summer flowers.

Foliage plants should not be overlooked for lack of blossoms. Foliage plants anchor the garden in spring, summer and fall. They are able to conceal leggy stems and give rest for the eye from vast displays of vibrant colors. Foliage plants also add much color to the garden, and yes, green is a color! Green color palettes are calming and restful and can create their own version of a colorful garden. Mixing shades of green—chartreuse with blue-greens and dark greens— creates an interesting color display all on its own.

There is also a large selection of foliage plants which display stunning coloration. The best summer foliage annual is Coleus *(Solenostemon)* which offers bright yellow, dark burgundy and orange-apricot leaves, many with multiple colors on a single leaf. Perennials such as the Coral Bell family *(Heuchera),* boast purple, yellow, and apricot foliage as well as others with variegation. Barberry *(Berberis thunbergii* 'Rose Glow'*)* has leaves marbled with wine, pink and white. Other shrubs in the Barberry family display golden or deep purple foliage. Large Red Maple *(Acer platanoides* 'Crimson King'*)* and smaller Japanese Maple *(Acer palmatum f. atropurpureum)* flaunt red-purple foliage all summer long.

Summer Garden Schedule
JULY/AUGUST
Mow lawns at two and a half to three inches to encourage deeper roots
Water lawns only as needed; one inch per week is sufficient to sustain grass
Dead head faded flowers to encourage more blooms and tidier plant appearance
Fertilize container plants; water daily
Monitor insect damage and apply natural control measures
Cultivate gardens to eliminate weeds
Water gardens as needed
Take cuttings from deciduous shrubs to start new plants

71

Fushcia (*Fushcia procumbens* 'Rufus'), Yellow bells (*Cordyalis lutea*), Spiderwort *(Tradescantia andersoniana)*
Friendship Plant (*Pilea involucrate*), Fushcia (*Fushcia fulgrens*), Swedish Ivy (*Plectanthus forsteri* 'Marginatus')
Ornamental Onion (*Allium giganteum*), Daylily (*Hemerocallis* 'Limelight'), Flowering Maple (*Abutilon pictum*)

Fall Gardens

As the sun begins to lose its warmth and days become shorter, the bountiful summer blossoms are replaced with another show; less bestowed with flowers, yet stunning all the same. The Master's paintbrush has touched the trees and shrubs, showing their glorious colors like no other season. Our gardens are filled with brilliant reds, vibrant oranges and luminous yellows. Green trees that shaded us in summer impress us with their dazzling fall attire before they shed their garb for winter.

Some summer perennial bloomers will carry over well into the fall. Many varieties of Roses *(Rosa)* will bloom until there is a covering of snow on the ground. Others, such as Black Eye Susan *(Rudbeckia)*, Coneflower *(Echinacea)*, and Large Sedum *(Sedum spectibile)* will push their way through fall, fading before the end of October. Still other perennials were meant especially for fall flowers. Mums *(Chrysanthemum)*, Toad Lily *(Tricyrits)*, Asters *(Aster)*, and Hibiscus *(Hibiscus moscheutos)* begin flowering as the nights become cool and give up their blossoms only after the most severe late fall frost.

Shrubs have mostly given up their flowers in favor of colorful foliage with the exception of Blue Mist Shrub *(Caryopteris)* which bares pale to dark blue or purple flower clusters for most of the autumn. Spirea *(Spiraea bumalda)*, *(Spiraea japonica)* will also give a secondary floral show in September if pruned shortly after its blooming period in July.

Annuals will shrivel up one by one as the temperature drops, but there are a few that will withstand a great deal of frost and may even bloom for a short period after the first snow. Blue Salvia *(Salvia farinacea* 'Victoria'*)*, Snapdragon *(Antirrhinum)*, and Pansy *(Viola x wittrockiana)* are all unwilling to yield to winter too soon.

Delight in Seasons

Benmiller Inn, Benmiller ON

Chapter Four

74

Fall Garden Schedule

SEPTEMBER	OCTOBER
Cease any fertilization of garden plants or shrubs to prevent soft new growth which may be killed off in winter	Take advantage of fall sales for major tree and shrub purchases
Fertilize trees	Plant spring bulbs
Plant new lawn areas, over seed any thinning lawn	Cut back perennials
Divide perennials	Remove annual plants
Prepare and plant new gardens	Apply tree wraps to young trees
Collect and dry seeds for use the following growing season	Mow over fallen leaves several times to chop finely; blow into garden beds or place in composter
Plant spring bulbs	Tie or cover up evergreens susceptible to snow damage
Mow lawn at two to two and a half inches	Hill roses

GLORY IN COLOR

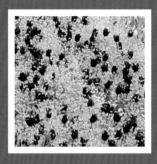

"When I see the rainbow in the clouds,

I will remember the eternal covenant between God

and every living creature on earth."

Genesis 9:16 NLT

Butchart Gardens, Central Saanich BC

God has filled this earth with extravagant color. Every inch of the earth is covered with color, from the green of the earth's floor and the turquoise of tropical seas to his rainbow spread across the dark grey sky. All of nature between the sea and the sky has been lavishly splashed with every color and shade imaginable. God's continued promise of mercy is renewed each time we see his rainbow, His gracious gift of color.

Color can be used to create a particular mood within a garden. It has the ability to stimulate and excite or to calm and soothe. When entering a garden, the first thing noticed is generally color. It is important to know how to appropriately and effectively use color in your garden.

Chapter Five

Warm Colors, Cool Colors

Warm colors are composed of those in the red zone of the color wheel and include orange, pink, and magenta. Warm colors are stimulating, and intense warm colors, such as red, are known to increase heart rate and release adrenaline. Cool colors produce a calming sensation. Cool colors include blue and those with blue undertones, such as purple and green. Incorporating too much strong color without visual relief may become overwhelming. Bright, warm, intense colors appear softened when paired with a cool color. Cool colors may be used without restraint in a garden since they are restful to the eye. Strong warm colors are best used as focal points and accents within the garden.

Warm colors appear to advance and well-placed warm accents can make a large garden appear more contained. A garden that is short but wide will appear squarer if bright colors are used on each side. A long corridor will appear shorter if a large urn filled with bright orange annuals or a trellised climbing red rose is placed at its end. Colorful built structure is even more effective in achieving these perceptions because it maintains its appearance regardless of the season. Brightly colored lattice work or fencing on each side

Butchart Gardens, Central Saanich BC

Glory in Color

Chapter Five

of a wide garden will make it appear narrower; in the same way, a brightly painted gate at the end of a narrow corridor will make the corridor appear shorter. The opposite is also true. Cool colors planted or painted on the sides of a narrow garden will result in a wider appearance. A short garden will be visually lengthened if white flowers are planted at the garden's end.

Color Harmony

At the close of winter, each gardener anticipates the joyous trip to the garden center to discover all of the new and improved plant varieties on the market. The hardest thing for a gardener to do, novice or professional, is to carefully choose which plants to tuck away into the trunk of our car. It is important to use restraint and only purchase plants which will enhance the color harmony we have established in our gardens rather than just any plant that catches our fancy. Harmony within the garden is best obtained by selecting just a few colors instead of including all of the colors available. In large gardens with several garden rooms, a new color theme may be introduced in each area.

Choosing your color harmony will depend on the colors in the architecture of your home, your personality,

and what purpose you will be using each section of the garden for. The plants you choose to place closest to your home should complement the colors on the building. Feel free to be more liberal with your color choice as you move away from your home. A very outgoing person is more likely to choose an intense color palette. Bright yellows, deep purples, and shocking reds would be their probable choices. A subdued personality will probably be drawn to a subtle contrast palette of soft

Royal Botanical Gardens, Burlington ON

pinks, mauves, and whites. While a monochromatic palette further limits the choice of plants within the garden, it is a color combination that has great strength and is very easy to pull together. A monochromatic approach is pleasing to both the outgoing and the more subdued personality. In the monochromatic scheme there will be a single color in a variety of tints and tones supported by the green of the foliage. An orange combination, for instance, would have the palest apricot, a warm tangerine, the most intense pumpkin color and every shade available in between. The variance in the intensity of the colors makes a very pleasing, welcoming garden.

Color Jumping

Unity within the garden is very dependant on the placement of color. Various colors scattered throughout the garden without regard to placement can cause a garden to lose its sense of unity. Repeating a color in specific spaces through the whole of the garden will guide your eye to "jump" from one spot to another and allows you to see the garden collectively. It is not necessary to use the same variety of plant from one spot to the next, but it does need to be of a similar color and intensity. Since various plants have different blooming schedules, it is important to jump plants with similar bloom times. This also means that you may have a different color dominate your garden in different seasons. April may be the yellow palette, May; blues and purples, June may fill your garden with pink flowers, red for July and August, and oranges may transform your gardens in September and October. Each season will include other colors as well, but the eye will first be drawn to the dominant color which skips through your gardens.

Lynne & Brian Bishop, Goderich ON

Mass Planting

When planting your garden, consider the quantity of like plants you will be using in each area of the garden. Various colors in the garden appear best when planted en masse. Large collections or swaths of the same color encourage unity within the garden, just as color jumping does. Single plants scattered throughout the garden, even if they are placed with regard to color jumping, gives the garden a polka dotted look. Significant color blocks create instant impact and heightened interest. The size of your mass plantings will be dependant on both the size of your garden and the size of the plant. A very large lilac *(syringa)*, can stand on its own. An annual such as a begonia will need many plants in order to have any visual interest at all. A small garden can often have groupings of three to

APRIL	MAY	JUNE	JULY & AUGUST	SEPTEMBER & OCTOBER
Daffodils *Narcissus*	Giant Onion *Allium gigantium*	Bulb Lily *Lilium* Asiatic	Lucifer Lily *Crocosmia*	Fall Mums *Chrysanthemum*
Bulb Iris *Iris reticulate*	Rhizomus Iris *Iris Laevigatae*	Peony *Paeonia*	Phlox, *Phlox paniculata*	Chinese Lanterns *Physalis alkekengi*
Crocus *Crocus*	Forget-me-nots *Myosotis*	Sea Pinks *Armeria*	Geranium *Pelargonium*	Skyracer Grass *Molina 'Skyracer'*
Forsythia *Forsythia*	Lilac *Syringa*	Deutzia *Deutzia gracilis*	Roses *Rosa*	Service Berry *Amelanchier*

five midsize plants, while this collection would get lost in a large garden. Large gardens can host seven, nine, or even fifteen of the same plant in one location. This is not to say there should be no singly planted specimens at all amongst the masses. Striking single plants are points of surprise and interest in every great garden. However, mass planting should be the majority of your garden with single plants used less extensively and chosen to create special points of interest or contrast.

Night Gardens

A garden has a completely different look in the evening than it does during the day. Colors that are brilliant become more restrained when darkness settles in. Colors that were subdued come to life and sparkle in the moonlight. The best colors for an evening garden are very light in color. White almost glows; light pinks and pale yellows appear brighter. Foliage streaked with white will also capture the lights at night. Flowers which surround a patio that is often used at night will benefit from the inclusion of a selection of white and very light colored flowers and foliage. Garden art that is white in color will make a wonderful focal point in the evening garden. White marble statuary or cast iron urns painted white will appear to jump out of a foliage filled garden.

Abkhazi Gardens, Victoria BC

83

Chapter Five

Color Interest for All Seasons

When we think of all of the beautifully colored flowers that will blanket our gardens in the warm season, it is important to remember that we need to have good foliage color to anchor our gardens when the flowers fall. Reminding ourselves to include sufficient evergreens, colored branches, and groundcover plantings will assure color in our gardens all twelve months of the year. It is also important to recall that perennials have a limited bloom time and that their foliage needs to carry the color interest when it is not in bloom. You may also wish to choose a plant for the foliage coloration rather than the blossom it may offer.

Although we are able to express our creativity in planning a garden, get lots of exercise in planting a garden and prove our work ethic in maintaining a garden, I believe the greatest joy in having a garden is the ability to surround ourselves in color with absolute abandon. I am ever so joyful that God chose to create this world; not in black in white, but filled with his glorious color.

Coleus 'Black Dragon' (*Solanostemon* 'Black Dragon'), Pototo Vine (*Ipomoea* 'Marguerite'), Knotweed (*Persacaria virginiana* 'Painter's Palette')
Blue Fescue (*Festuca glauca*), Ligularia (*Ligularia tussilaginea* 'Argentia Albo Marginata'), Blue Hosta (*Hosta* 'Blue Moon')

WONDER AT CO-CREATION

"The land produced vegetation; plants bearing seed according to their kinds and trees bearing fruit with seed in it according to their kinds. And God saw that it was good."

Genesis 1:12 NIV

Butchart Gardens, Central Saanich BC

God had this wonderful plan to include humankind in his creations. Although God is the only one who can actually create anything, we have been invited into the process. We are not in any way equal to God the Creator, but are his vessels for some of the creation process. We have learned to hybridize plants by crossing within the genus and recrossing again with cultivars. We have been able to recognize mutations and sports, which is a congested growth or a shoot varying from the rest of the plant, and cultivate them into new plants of their own.

Milner Gardens and Woodland, Qualicum Beach BC

Chapter Six

Hybridizing

How many plant species were in the Garden of Eden? We don't know, but ever since creation, humankind has been cross breeding plant species to create new varieties. This co-creation gift God has given us has given birth to an immense collection of

The rose, for instance, began with 150 species that we know of, probably more. Today there are many thousands of varieties of roses due to sports, mutations, and crosses with other roses. The species rose has five-petaled blossoms in spring followed by rose hips in the fall and winter. The species rose *(Rosa gal-*

whom so many of our hybrid roses come from today.

The same is true of most plant varieties that we are now blessed with. Almost all have gone through cultivation practices to give us an abundance of quality plant varieties to choose from for our gardens today.

plants. Species of plants have been hybridized to develop large collections of plants within a single genus. Each hybrid is created to improve on one or all of these qualities: growth, vigour, and habit; disease resistance, drought tolerance, hardiness; foliage and flower size, color, quantity, form, and fragrance.

lica), sometimes called *(Rosa rubra)* or the Red Rose, was cultivated by the Medes and Persians as early as the twelfth century BC. *Rosa gallica* was one of the parents of the well-known Apothecary Rose *(Rosa gallica officinalis)*, which has been used for medicinal purposes for centuries and is the parent from

Before cultivated plants are introduced into the market place, they must go through several seasons of growth to be sure they will maintain the characteristics they were bred for. Breeders who rush to get their new plant introduction on the market without taking the proper time to see how it performs over a long

Milner Gardens and Woodland, Qualicum Beach BC

period of time may disappoint buyers if the plant later displays poor performance.

Some plants have a tendency to revert back to the qualities of its parent plant. Plants with variegated or golden foliage, taken as sports from a wholly green plant, may over time revert back to entirely green appearance. A Harlequin Maple *(Acer platanoides* 'Drummondii') for instance, has a green leaf with a white edge, but occasionally a completely green-foliaged shoot may appear. If the green shoot is not cut out, the entire tree, over time, will revert back to a green-foliaged maple.

Seed collected from annuals results in a beautiful display the following summer. However, oftentimes the plants are bearing blossoms of a different color than the previous season. Seed collected from a pink Zinnia *(Zinnia),* may become a bed of pink, white, yellow, and red Zinnias the following year.

Hybrids may also cross pollinate so that eventually all same-species plants in a small area will bear the same color flowers. When pink and white Obedient Plant *(Physostegia lamiaceae),* are placed close to each other in a planting bed the pink may completely disappear leaving only white blossoms.

Cross Breeding

Cross breeding is when pollen is collected from the stamen of one plant and is brushed on the stigma

Wonder at Co-creation

of another of the same genus. It is important to remove the stamen of the receptive plant to avoid having the plant pollinate itself with its own pollen. When the plant produces seed, it will be a cross between the pollinating plant and the seed-bearing plant. The seed is then grown onto a mature plant where seed is collected and cuttings are taken and then grown onto more mature plants having qualities of both of the host plants. Many crosses are made and discarded before one successful new plant is introduced with the desirable qualities the breeder is seeking.

Mutations

Mutations occur as an accident during the formation of the seed during cross breeding. The chains of chromosomes on which the genes are carried can be disrupted so that one chain has an extra link while the other has fewer. The link may also be turned back on itself, breaking up the normal sequence arrangement. Also, the normal cell walls may be defective resulting in no cell division at all. All of these will cause a mutation and if the mutation can successfully mate, it becomes a new hybrid. Mutations create plants which are a complete surprise to the breeder.

Hatley Park National Historic Site, Victoria BC

Sports and Witches' Brooms

Sports or Witches' Brooms, on the other hand, are found as an oddity or unusual growth on a plant. A sport or witch's broom is a spontaneous development that is atypical to the rest of the plant. Sports are different from mutations in that they occur naturally and can only be reproduced vegetatively, not by seed. The sport is removed from the host plant and reproduced by cuttings or grafting. Many plants we have are a result of sports discovered and cultivated. A popular example is the Dwarf Alberta Spruce *(Picea glauca var. albertiana* 'Conica'). This spruce is a fine-needled miniature tree with perfect pyramidal form. Professor J. G. Jack and Alfred Rehder of the Arnold Arboretum discovered, collected, and cultivated this sport as a young seedling growing in Alberta near Lake Laggan. Many variegated plants have also been cultivated from such discoveries.

Thanks be to God who keeps us constantly in awe over his creation. Not only are we able to enjoy the plant material that surrounds us today, we may anticipate the new and exciting cultivars coming our way tomorrow. Now if only we were able to incorporate all of our favorite plants, old and new, into the limited boundaries of our gardens! Perhaps our inability to do so gives us the excuse and opportunity to be ever wandering into public gardens and our neighbors' back yards.

Wonder at Co-creation

EMBRACE CREATURES

"I know every bird in the mountains,

and the creatures of the field are mine."

Psalm 50:11 NIV

Filberg Heritage Lodge and Park, Comox BC

When we think of a garden, a beautiful oasis comes to mind where lush foliage abides, gorgeous, colorful flowers spring forth and sounds of bubbling waters and rustling grasses are heard. We can see ourselves sitting peacefully in this environment enjoying a good book and an equally good glass of wine.

Such an oasis, however, is made even better when it is also a place where butterflies flit by, humming birds pause to drink in the nectar of nearby blossoms and chipmunks scurry about storing food for winter. We are blessed when we are lulled to sleep by the low croak of a bullfrog and awakened to the tune of birds' songs. After all, God's original intention was for us to live alongside his creatures.

Attracting Birds

Shelter and Protection

Song birds search for a place where they feel secure from predators and extreme weather conditions, as well as a location where they can build their nests. *"Even the sparrow has found a home, and the swallow a nest for herself, where she may have her young" Psalm 84:3b NIV.* Birds like to hide in evergreens and nest in the boughs of foliage filled trees. Evergreens are especially necessary when we wish to attract winter song birds and are a must in our garden. Large evergreen trees such as Pine *(Pinus)*, Fir *(Abies)*, and Spruce *(Picea)* allow the birds to sit high and unexposed from predators and shelters them in cold winter storms.

Smaller evergreens such as Junipers *(Juniperus)*, Cedars *(Thuja)*, and Yews *(Taxus)* are also favorite nesting sites. Any evergreen is a valued protection and nesting place for all birds in your garden. Summer song birds that migrate south in winter will be equally satisfied with any deciduous trees with a full foliage canopy.

Hatley Park National Historic Site, Victoria BC

Lynne and Brian Bishop, Goderich ON

A bird house is the best way to attract hole-nesting birds, such as wrens, flickers, bluebirds, purple martins, chickadees and woodpeckers. Be sure your house is designed to fit the type of bird you wish to occupy it and is located where the bird feels most secure. Wrens choose houses that are small and have entrance holes no larger than one and a quarter inch. Purple martins like condominium type housing with several compartments and entrance holes. Most birds prefer their homes to be firmly anchored to a post or tree. Clean out houses either after the hatching season or before birds arrive in the springtime.

Water Sources

Birds need to preen and keep their feathers in top condition. Birds are happy to splash about in water puddles from spring rains. Rains, however, are not reliable and a ready supply of water will be appreciated. You will find that they will flock to a bird bath or a small water feature for refreshment and their regular baths.

Bird baths should be situated in open areas, but close enough to trees and shrubs that they will feel there is a quick escape should a predator harass them. Bird baths should be cleaned and filled regularly.

Food Provision

Birds will check out the whole neighborhood for the best diner, and if you have great food bearing plants as well as stocked feeders, they will be sure to pick yours. Offer an array of foods to attract a wide variety of birds.

Nature's plants are a bird's best source for nourishing meals. The widest food choice will come from a variety of seed, nectar and fruit producing species. Trees, shrubs, perennials and annuals all provide either berries or seeds.

If you decide to provide additional food for birds, there are many possibilities. For the main course offer a good quality seed mix containing a variety of seed. Place the mix in any type of hanging or post feeder.

Author's Garden, Goderich ON

Embrace Creatures

Offer tasty side dishes to lure particular birds. A selection of sunflowers will attract cardinals, jays, grosbeaks and pine siskins. Niger or thistle seed is a favorite of pine siskins and a variety of finches. Niger seed can be placed in special cylinder feeders or fine mesh bags hung from tree branches. Woodpeckers and nuthatches have a taste for suet and many other birds will eat it on occasion. Beef suet can be purchased

usually contain artificial food colorants as an attractant. Birds are equally satisfied with a homemade mixture of one part sugar to four parts water without any additives. If your feeder is made of orange or red glass or plastic or has brightly colored feeding stations, that will be sufficient to draw these types of birds.

Round out the meal by serving a dessert of bits of fresh fruit in hol-

part melted beef suet. Spoon into lined muffin cups and harden in the refrigerator. For a ready supply, hardened cakes may be placed in a sealed container and placed in a cool location until ready for use.

Birds are appreciative of a supply of food throughout the year, but also may become dependent on it. Birds will find other places to feed in the summer if your supply runs out, but

Holly (*Ilex meservea*); Crab Apple (*Malus* 'Butterball'); Mountain Ash (*Sorbus aucuparia*)

from your butcher and stuffed in meshed bags (onion or produce bags work well) or in a wire basket. Fasten the bag or basket to the side of a tree or on a feeder pole.

Humming bird feeders filled with sugar water will make you popular with hummingbirds, tanagers, grosbeaks, orioles and warblers. Commercial mixes can be purchased but

lowed citrus or melon halves. Thrushes, orioles and warblers will become loyal visitors to your backyard.

All birds delight in bird cakes. Commercial cakes are available for purchase; however it is fun and easy to make your own. Mix one part peanut butter, two parts mixed birdseed and five parts cornmeal to one

may perish during winter if your food supply suddenly ceases. For this reason it is especially important to keep your feeders full at all times during the winter.

Favorite Avian Cuisine					
Bird	Sunflower Seed	Niger Seed	Beef Suet	Whole Corn	Peanut Butter
Blue Jay	*		*	*	*
Cardinal	*			*	
Chickadee	*	*	*		*
Evening Grosbeak	*				
Flicker			*		*
Gold finch	*	*			
House Finch	*	*			*
Junco	*				*
Mourning Dove				*	
Nuthatch	*		*		*
Pine Siskin		*			
Purple Finch	*	*			
Starling			*		
Siskin					*

ATTRACTING BUTTERFLIES

Butterflies are graceful, colorful living flowers. They add movement to our gardens and are one of the few insects that we actively encourage to inhabit our gardens. Most butterflies join us for a time and then move on. Other butterflies delight us throughout the warm season and choose to lay their eggs nearby. If your home is situated in a rural area or adjacent

a stream, swamp or deciduous forest butterflies are nearby, ready to be lured into your garden. An urban dweller will have to plan a little more carefully to attract a host of butterflies.

To encourage the largest selection of butterflies, we need to feed the caterpillar and larvae as well as the butterfly. It is necessary to research the types of butterflies that frequent your geographical region so you will know

Embrace Creatures

what plants will best suit the butterflies you are attempting to attract.

Butterflies are appreciative of sheltered locations for wind protection and open sunny spaces in which to sun. Butterflies do not fly well when their body temperature is under 70 fahrenheit (21celcius). They are unable to internally regulate their body temperature and therefore rely on the warmth of the sun. Butterflies can often be seen basking on rocks on

vorite plant of any butterfly is the Butterfly Bush *(Buddleja).* Even one of these honey scented shrubs will attract the most discerning of butterflies. Over ripened fruit such as citrus, bananas, peaches and plums can be offered as well.

Butterflies like to lay their eggs in sheltered areas such as shrubs or in brush piles where their pupa will be safe from excessive wind and rains. The larvae and caterpillars feed on

home in your garden.

Special care should also be afforded the butterflies in your garden. To keep flourishing populations in your garden avoid all insecticides. Also, enjoy the butterflies just with your eyes, not your hands. Delicate wings are easily damaged when handled. If you find a chrysalis, move it while attached to the twig to a sheltered, shaded location where you can watch the butterfly emerge. It is

Butterfly Weed (*Asciepias tuberosa*) ; Milkweed (*Asclepias incarnata*); Butterfly Bush (*Buddlija davidii*)

cool mornings to warm up before flight. For this reason you will see many more butterflies active on warm sunny days than on cooler overcast days.

Large groupings of nectar producing plants are more likely to invite butterflies than those which are planted singly. The absolute fa-

foliage rather than nectar. Including a variety of trees, grasses and certain weed plants will encourage your butterfly population to stick around.

After a rainfall butterflies can be seen drinking from shallow puddles. A damp area in the garden or a dish filled with rocks and water will also help butterflies feel at

most amazing how God turns a lowly caterpillar into a colorful, living flower.

Not So Welcome Guests

While we welcome birds and butterflies, there is mixed opinion on many of the other creatures that may wander through our gardens. Rabbits de-

Embrace Creatures

Filberg Heritage Lodge and Park, Comox BC

light as they hop about, but can discourage us when they have eaten many of our treasured plants. The same can be said for deer. They can be a joy to see but they may leave severely trimmed plants in their wake. Blue herons are magnificent birds; however, they may appear a little less grand when they are gulping down your prized koi fish. Even in Solomon's time he spoke of four footed creatures that ruined his gardens. *"Catch for us the foxes, the little foxes that ruin the vineyards, our vineyards that are in bloom." Song of Songs 2:15 NIV.* And so it is still today.

When living in a rural area or adjacent to a forest, you have little choice but to rejoice in the creatures that come to call. I, for one, feel so very blessed to be able to watch a deer and its fawn drink from my pond regardless of the fact that my magnolias bloom only at the top and tulips are no longer an option in my garden. The blue herons that come to feast on a fish dinner are really controlling my overpopulated pond. Bunnies devouring my plants, chipmunks planting walnuts everywhere, and squirrels digging up the spring bulbs I've just planted…well, some days I'm not so sure about them.

Summer is a time of plenty for most animals that like to share our garden space. They are usually content to share our garden without lunching on anything but a bit of our lawn's grass. But when snow covers the ground and their usual food source becomes scarce, particularly in late winter and early spring, they may cause a great deal of damage to our trees and ornamental plants. There is little that can be done for protec-

necessary to protect it from other creatures in the deepest snow conditions. Shrubs may be wrapped with burlap or circled with snow fencing.

Squirrels and chipmunks like to dig up our newly planted spring bulbs. Small areas planted with bulbs can be protected by placing chicken wire over the bulbs before they are cov-

in our garden.

Other than barrier protection, there is little we can do to deter rabbits, chipmunks and squirrels short of erecting an impenetrable fence. We can, however, limit the damage done in our gardens by deer. They may continue to wander about delighting at the dawn of the day without reek-

Milner Gardens and Woodland, Qualicum Beach BC

Butchart Gardens, Central Saanich BC

tion other than covering susceptible plants. Tree guards will protect the bark of young trees from foraging deer, mice and rabbits. It is essential to wrap the tree trunk about two inches below grade to protect it from mice and voles and as high up as

ered with soil. These spunky animals are also in the habit of hiding acorns and walnuts throughout our gardens. The following growing season we are left with the task of pulling out the saplings which seem to have sprouted almost everywhere

ing havoc on our gardens. Choosing to plant only things that they will not eat and deciding to enjoy expanses of daffodils rather than tulips will help to create harmony with God's creatures once again.

CELEBRATE UNIQUENESS

"I praise you because I am fearfully and wonderfully made;

your works are wonderful, I know that full well."

Psalm 139:14 NIV

Niagra Parks, Niagra Falls ON

God has filled the world with so many wonderful things and has blessed us with various senses to enjoy them with. God has wired everyone differently; therefore we each experience things in our own unique way. We were each created with different abilities and needs. This is true of each stage of our life from youth to aged and the way in which we experience things will change throughout our life. God created some of us with more limited abilities than others. Others may experience permanent injuries due to accidents or diminished abilities caused by disease or aging. Gardens can be tailored to accommodate every person regardless of what physical limitations they may have. Not only can each person enjoy being in a garden, but most people with physical limitations can also be part of its creation and maintenance. However God made you, you can enjoy the beauty of a garden.

Butchart Gardens, Central Saanich BC

Chapter Eight

GARDENS FOR THE VISUALLY IMPAIRED

A garden is not just about how it appears; it is also about how it may be experienced through our other senses. Oftentimes when a person cannot see, their other senses become more acute. A well planned garden can therefore be a wondrous place for the visually impaired. Taking time to focus on tactile plants and materials, including elements that perk your ears, inviting the song of birds and frogs, adding a snippet of something to taste, and surrounding the garden in scent is to truly create a garden to experience.

Touch

You can experience touch through many mediums in a garden setting. Choosing tactile plants, those with fine textures, furry surfaces and rough peeling layers are essential to a garden which will be felt. It is equally important, however, to pay attention to the textures of the fencing, walls, art and furniture which adorn the garden.

Opposing textures in juxtaposing placements capture interest and heighten each individual texture. A Maiden Hair Fern *(Adiantum)* nestled under a large, puckered leaf Hosta *(Hosta* 'Frances Williams') placed beside smooth rockery gives a variety of textures in a very small site.

When designing a planting plan for a garden with texture in mind it is important to carry various textures through the seasons. In much of North America we experience as many months without the benefit of gardens overflowing with flowers as we do with. Include evergreen plants, trees and shrubs with twisted, peeling or gnarly bark. Interesting grasses and perennials with lasting seed heads will also extend the enjoyment of the garden into even the bleakest months of the year.

Be sure to avoid any plants which may be prickly, such as Holly *(Ilex)* or Juniper *(Juniperus)* or any plant which may cause skin irritation or dermatitis when touched.

109

Kitty Coleman Woodland Gardens, Victoria BC

Pondsview Garden Centre, Goderich ON

Garden art can take on many forms, from smooth and slick to grooved and textured. Various materials—metal, concrete, stone, wicker, wood, and glass—all serve to interest the "feeler" with unique and opposing experiences. Hands can also pass over sculpture to reveal recognizable shapes and patterns.

Consider the placement and color of your art to achieve sharply contrasting temperatures. Dark colors absorb the sun's rays and warmth while cool colors reflect the sun's rays. A concrete planter placed in the shade will feel very cool to the touch, while warmth will radiate from a black wrought iron planter in full sun.

Fences, pergolas and arbours can be made with a variety of materials. Wattle fences composed of twigs woven through rough wooden posts are highly textural, while a wrought iron fence is smooth in texture, but may have an interesting pattern forged into its design, which can be explored with hands.

Water, while often considered more for its soothing sounds, is another element offering a unique tactile experience. A hand caressed by a foaming fountain, or fingertips cooled by water in a still birdbath, add just one more dimension to a garden for the visually impaired.

Taste

Ornamental gardens may also include a smattering of edible plants. Fruit trees offer not only cherries and peaches, but a wonderful floral show in the spring. Many fruiting bushes are appealing to the eye as well as the palette. Currant and blueberry bushes and grapevines contribute colorful fruit to the garden. Cherry tomatoes, peppers and herbs mix well in and amongst perennials.

Celebrate Uniqueness

Hyacinth (*Hyacinthus orientalis*); Daphne (*Daphne cneorum*); Snowball bush (*Viburnum carlcephalum*)
Thyme (*Thymus vulgaris*); Nastursium (*Nastursium*); Viola (*Viola*)
Lambs ears (*Stachys Byzantina*); Chenille Plant (*Amaranthus caudatus*); Spurge (*Euphorbia myrsinites*)

The Governors House Gardens, Victoria BC

Many flowers are also good for the palette. Pansies *(Violas)* and Nasturtiums *(Tropaeolum)* make colorful and flavorful additions to salads and garnishes to entrées. Nasturtium seeds are also a good substitute for capers. Daylilies *(Hemerocallis)* taste similar to lettuce and are a great salad accompaniment or a unique addition to a stir fry. Apple, peach and pear blossoms have a delicate flavor and are a good pairing with fresh fruit salads or as garnishes. Carnations *(Dianthus)*, Lavender *(Lavandula)* and Roses *(Rosa)* are delicious mixed into custards or ice cream dishes. Brightly colored petals of any edible flower are attractive when frozen into ice cubes and used to cool drinks on a hot summers' day.

It is essential to consider placement of edible flowers in a visually impaired garden. They need to be separate from the remainder of the ornamental plantings so there can be no mistake when picking and eating the flower petals. It is also important to be sure no chemicals were used on the flowers intended for eating. For this reason you should never eat flowers purchased from a florist or garden centre or from the side of the road, as many of these would have been sprayed with chemicals during their growth cycle.

The best time to pick your edible flowers is in the early morning as that is when they have the highest moisture content. Remove the pistil and stamens and only eat the flowers petals.

While it is the foliage of most edible herbs that is usually used in culinary dishes, their flowers are also useful in a variety of dishes. The flowers generally have a slightly milder taste than the foliage but should be included for their visual appeal. Placing herbs close to your kitchen door will invite you to include them regularly in your favorite dishes.

Sound

An often-forgotten dimension of our garden is the presence of sound. Subtle garden sounds can be orchestrated by the rustle of wind passing through plant material, objects that

113

jingle in the breeze, the presence of moving water and the introduction of plants and structures which attract birds and frogs.

Prior to plant placement think about where the wind will blow the most. Tall grasses and bamboos that will rustle should be positioned in the wind's path.

Whether listening to the crash of water cascading onto rocks, hearing the gentle trickle of water from an earthen jar or absorbing the sound of a gurgling stream, water plays an elemental role in a garden. For the visually impaired, water in a garden is essential. Daily stresses and anxieties are carried away by the sound of the water's flow.

A true surprise is how quickly frogs find their way to a newly dug pond or water feature. Big bullfrogs will echo their calls from the water's edge and spring peepers will send out their lullaby as you drift off to sleep. Toads can be invited to call your garden home when you include a toad house. Toad houses may be purchased, but a clay pot placed on its side planted half way in the ground in a shady, moist area is a sufficient home for a toad. The added benefit of frogs and toads is the copious amount of insects they can consume each day.

Birds need several things to feel secure before they will fill your garden with song. They look for protection from predators and extreme weather conditions, a food source and bathing sites. A great garden will include evergreens for birds to hide in, berry producing trees and shrubs, seed bearing perennials and grasses, and a bird bath, pond or waterfall. Additional bird houses and feeders will ensure even more birds choose your garden.

Wind chimes give off different tones depending on their material and size. Wood or bamboo emits a low, clunking noise, metal a higher, sharper sound, and glass a tinkling, gentle jingle.

Introducing sounds from water fea-

Pondsview Garden Centre, Goderich ON

Butchart Gardens, Central Saanich BC

Butchart Gardens, Central Saanich BC

Celebrate Uniqueness

tures and wind chimes can also help to mask undesirable sounds. Noises created by passing traffic, neighboring families or from manufacturing plants become less apparent when your garden includes more pleasant sounds close to your seating area.

When plants, creatures, water features, and sound-producing objects are used in combination, the garden becomes a feast for the ears.

Scent

The breath of a fragrant flower is oftentimes more magnificent than the sight of its blossom. Many subtly scented flowers release their aroma when trodden under foot or when brushed against. Other plants infuse the air more substantially in the dewy, still of the evening. A gentle breeze can send the perfume from the simplest of flowers far from where it is situated. *"Awake north wind, and come, south wind! Blow on my garden, that its fragrance may spread abroad." Song of Songs 4:16 NIV*

Situating your aromatic plants is key to extracting the most fragrance from them. An arbor bedecked with Hall's Honeysuckle *(Lonicera japonica* 'Halliana'*)* or Sweet Autumn Clematis *(Clematis terniflora paniculata)* will fragrance not only the air as you stroll through, but the whole of the surrounding area as well. A Lavender *(Lavandula)* hedge alongside a narrow path will release an added measure of perfume when brushed against. Walking over varieties of Thyme *(Thymus)* inserted between flagstones in a casual pathway will emit the essential oils so the aroma may waft upwards. Shrubs such as Daphne *(Daphne)* are best planted close to where you will be sitting so you may enjoy its intoxicating fragrance. Lilac *(Syringa)* on the other hand, can be planted many yards away from your patio and still be thoroughly enjoyed.

Including scented evergreens in your garden will increase the seasons of scent value. Cedar *(Thuja),* Spruce *(Picea),* and Pine *(Pinus)* all add aromatic interest year round, but are the staples of a scented winter garden. Winter flowering Witch Hazel *(Hamamelis x intermedia)* *(Hamamelis x mollis)* will add that feathery blossom in winter as well as a light hint of spice. Thyme *(Thymus)* will continue to spill out its scented oils even when walked upon in the cold of winter.

Gardens for Those with Limited Mobility

People with limited mobility, such as those who use a wheel chair, or those who have chronic back problems, can still participate in creating and maintaining their own garden. Taking the garden up off of the ground and into raised beds and planters cre-

MacNaughton Park, Exeter ON

Butchart Gardens, Central Saanich BC

ates accessible gardens for all.

Those who experience chronic back problems need to have gardens at levels where they may work without bending. Gardens need to be only as wide as can be comfortably reached from two sides. The ideal raised garden depends on a person's height, but for most adults a raised bed which is three to four feet tall is ideal. If a raised bed is accessible from both sides, it should not be wider than six and a half feet. Raised planters which have a wall behind them, should not be wider than three and a quarter feet. These dimensions will allow the gardener to work without straining their backs. For raised beds tailored specifically to the gardener, measure from under their arm to their hip. The gardener will experience the most comfort gardening within this range. Using specialized tools will also help access areas that are just out of reach. Pruning tools which have long handles will be helpful for pruning trees and shrubs as well as deadheading plants. Raising hose bibs to three to four feet high will eliminate bending over when it is time to water the garden.

A wheel chair friendly garden requires raised beds at a height of one and a half feet to three and a half feet.

Butchart Gardens, Central Saanich BC

Chapter Eight

Gardens should not be wider than four feet if accessible from both sides, and no more than two feet in width if located against a wall. Use of large containers is ideal for those in wheelchairs as they are easily able to reach into the container garden from all sides. Long handled pruning tools will also be an advantage to those using wheel chairs. Apart from creating accessible gardens to work in, it is also important to be sure a wheel chair can easily get to them. Grass, loose stone and wood chip surfaces can be uneven and difficult if not impossible to move around on. Ideal surfaces would be wood, interlock brick or concrete. All pathways from the house and around the gardens need to be of a hard surface and include ramps instead of stairs where necessary so the wheel chair can easily roll to every area.

Elderly people and those with Parkinson's disease, cerebral palsy and other conditions causing people to be unstable on their feet will also benefit from hard surfaces in garden areas.

Raised beds can be made of many materials. Your existing architecture, personal preference and budget will determine which material is right for you. If natural stone is your choice of material, using stone that comes from a quarry close to you will be your best choice financially as much of the cost

of stone comes from its transport. The benefit of stone is that it is a permanent fixture, and a properly installed raised bed will be there indefinitely. There are many cultured stone and brick products in a full range of prices, many of which are easily installed by a homeowner. Recycled rail ties or cedar rails are an economical choice and with proper installation will last for many years.

Long past are the days when containers were just meant to host annuals on your patio. Large, insulated containers are well suited to small evergreens and shrubs and even small trees. Perennials and grasses do equally well in containers. The key to successfully over wintering container gardens is container size and insulation. Plants die in containers not because of the winters cold but more often because of desiccating winds and the freeze/thaw cycles which happen frequently over winter.

Containers which hold a lot of soil and are insulated will prevent the freeze/thaw cycles from damaging tender roots. Containers need sufficient water before they freeze up so that evergreens are well hydrated. Use materials for your container which will not crack during winter. Wood, metal and polystyrene are good choices. There must be a drainage hole and an inch or two of

drainage stone on the bottom to prevent water logging precious plants. Beautiful polystyrene containers are available that mimic concrete, clay or cast iron in appearance. These containers are insulated due to the material they are made of. Any container can be winterized by placing one inch styrofoam on the bottom and around its perimeter or by applying spray foam inside the container and cutting it back to about an inch.

Additional success will be assured if you use plants that are at least one zone hardier than the zone you live in. Containers which are placed in wind alleys should be moved to a more sheltered location for the winter.

Containers planted with trees, shrubs or perennials will not have their soil changed, sometimes for many years. For this reason it is important to initially plant your container with a very good soil mixture. The soil needs to be fertile and provide good drainage while retaining sufficient water. A good mixture would consist of one part peat moss, one part composted sheep manure, one part perlite to four parts soiless mix. A top dressing of peat and manure can be added in spring and adding organic fertilizer or compost tea to an occasional watering will keep the plants healthy throughout the seasons.

Gardens for Children

The ideal garden for children is one where they are free to touch and explore. Tip toeing through a stepping stone path to hide under a shade tree or playing within a small hedged secret garden are adventures for small children. Including garden art that moves in the wind or sparkles in the sun will create a whimsical atmosphere for a child.

The most valuable part of a children's garden is the area where they are free to run and play. If you only have a small back yard, it is best to keep the manicured gardens to the front yard where you may enjoy them without fear of plants being trampled by little feet. The ideal small backyard children's garden would have a well branched tree for climbing and hanging a tire swing, enough green space to kick a soccer ball, a corner for a small play house and a sunny fence side to grow a few giant sunflowers.

If you are blessed with a large back yard, your options are limitless. You are able to create a fun garden for children where they can play, appreciate a wide variety of plants and learn about God's promises to them.

One idea for teaching young children God's truths through our gardens is to create a rainbow and Ark theme. By

Milner Gardens and Woodland, Qualicum Beach BC

Butchart Gardens, Central Saanich BC

using colors of the rainbow, plants with names of animals and a splashing water feature, the story of Noah and the flood will come alive.

The rainbow can be represented by the use of concrete pavers painted in bright rainbow colours to create a hop scotch through the garden. The rainbow can also be represented by multicoloured flags or colourful annuals planted in a rainbow pattern.

Several bird houses painted in bright primary colours encourage birds to live in your garden as well as present the rainbow promise.

A water feature or small wading pool with a fountain or water fall is a good reminder that even though God sent rain for forty days and forty nights, he has promised to never again destroy the whole earth with a flood.

It is important to not include any plants which may be poisonous if ingested or cause skin irritation, or dermatitis if touched. Foxglove *(Digitalis)* for instance, would be a great plant to include in an Ark-themed garden; however the whole plant can cause severe discomfort if ingested as well as cause skin irritation when contact has occurred with the foliage.

Gardens for the Developmentally Challenged

Those who are developmentally challenged are typically attracted to the same garden elements that children are. While missing the subtleties of finely textured foliage and tiny, pale blossoms, they celebrate flowers that are big, brash and bold, foliage that is unusually large or grasses that tower over them. Garden art that is either brightly colored or over scaled and wind chimes that shout out their tunes are sure to be hits with the developmentally challenged.

When creating a garden for developmentally challenged people, be prepared to throw out the rules of what a perfect garden should look like. Their garden should be all about what is fun and unconventional. They should be able to participate in its creation and maintenance. Whenever they are allowed to be participants rather than just onlookers, they will take ownership and feel like the garden is truly theirs.

When including developmentally challenged people in creating a garden, be sure that pathways are firm for those that may be less steady on their feet. Also, when choosing plant-

The Governors House Gardens, Victoria BC

ings, include fast growing seeds. There is no greater satisfaction than watching a seed grow into a beautiful plant. Use seeds that are large and easy to handle. Fine seeds are difficult to pick up and may become a frustration rather than a benefit.

Use plants that have brightly colored blossoms, especially those with red, orange, yellow and hot pink coloration. They will be attracted to any plant with bright colors, but especially to those that also bestow an unusually large flower.

When we plan and plant our garden for each person who will be regularly entering it, it will be a place where everyone feels at home. For those who face daily challenges in this world due to physical or cognitive limitations, the garden will be a haven where they know they are included. A place where they can participate, just as fully able bodied people may. It will become the true sanctuary that a garden should be; a little slice of Eden, God's perfect garden.

Pondsview Garden Centre, Goderich ON

REJOICE IN COMMUNITY

"Don't forget to show hospitality to strangers, for some who have done this have entertained angels without realizing it!"

Hebrews 13:2 NLT

Butchart Gardens, Central Saanich BC

God knew right from the beginning that it was not good for man to be alone. Not only did he give Eve to Adam, he directed them to multiply and fill the earth and he blessed them with children. People have been gathering together to celebrate, share meals and enjoy each other's companionship for millennia. Hospitality was so important in Bible times that to refuse to entertain a stranger was a sin. The new church in Acts *"shared their meals with great joy and generosity—all the while praising God and enjoying the goodwill of all the people." Acts 2:46-47 NLT*

We still yearn to be in fellowship with others. We were created to be communal people. We can use the gift of hospitality by creating gardens where our friends and family are welcomed. Our gardens can become places where people eat, play, and linger. We can have peaceful areas for conversation, gardens filled with easy-to-pick-up games, areas devoted to food preparation and dining, as well as fireplaces or fire pits where we may enjoy our guests long into the evening.

Butchart Gardens, Central Saanich BC

Chapter Nine

Garden Rooms

It is far preferable to live within a garden rather than simply look upon it. Instead of only dressing up the edges of your property or planting flower beds directly against your home, think about surrounding yourself with a variety of plants. A well thought out garden design can turn outdoor spaces into garden rooms – rooms which are an extension of your home's living and entertaining space. A well put together outdoor room will become a frequently used area for entertaining family and friends.

Plan your square footage well before you build a new patio or deck. Lay out furniture and cooking locations

Lynne & Brian Bishop, Goderich ON

on the ground before you begin. Knowing how much space you will need for your desired furniture and barbeque area will prevent regrets after construction is complete.

Choose a location for your patio that is convenient to your family room or kitchen entrance and allows you to have a sufficient amount of sunlight. Locating a patio with the sole consideration of shade protection is unnecessary as shade can easily be added to any outdoor room, whereas sun cannot.

Define your garden room's area by using walls, ceilings, and floors. It is possible to use only one of these elements in the creation of your room, but the more elements used, the more it will feel like an outdoor room.

Floors

The ground plane or floor is a very important part of your room. Choosing a material different from the ground alongside your room will define its space. Changing the elevation will also achieve the effect of entering another garden room. The material you use on your floor will depend on the architecture of your home and your budget. Economical choices include crushed, compacted gravel, precast concrete slabs, and flagstone laid on a gravel base. The benefit of choosing crushed gravel

Lynne & Brian Bishop, Goderich ON

when on a budget is that it can easily be overlaid with a more permanent hard surface in future when the budget permits. Each of these options can be self installed, saving substantially on installation costs. Using steppable plants between flagstone or concrete slabs creates a visually softer surface. Good choices that will withstand foot traffic include Thyme *(Thymus)*, Creeping Sedum *(Sedum subulata)*, and mosses such as Irish Moss *(Sagina subulata* 'Aurea'*)*. Higher cost patios are made from cedar or composite decking, concrete, which can be colored or textured, interlock brick or square-cut slate or flagstone. It is best to have professionals install the more expensive materials.

Walls

Garden walls enfold you; give you visual dimensions for your room, and offer privacy and shelter from the wind. Walls do not have to be high to be effective. An eighteen inch structure or hedge will give the illusion of a wall and effectively define the space.

Walls for your room can be borrowed from existing architecture such as the exterior wall of your home, garden shed or fence. Additional walls can be built structure such as a fence, trellis, arbor, stone or brick wall, or a series of columns. Such walls may be softened by clinging vines such as Climbing Hydrangea *(Hydrangea anomola petiolaris),* or Virginia Creeper *(Parthenocissus quinquefolia),* or trellised vines such as Climbing Rose *(Rosa* 'Climbing Iceberg'*)* or Honey Suckle *(Lonicera).*

Plant material is a good choice for walls as well. Low hedges of Boxwood *(Buxus),* or Fountain Grass *(Pennisetum alopecuroides),* medium-high hedges of Holly *(Ilex),* or Spirea *(Spiraea),* and tall hedges grown from Cedar *(Thuja),* or Rose of Sharon *(Hibiscus syriacus),* add color and sometimes fragrance to the room.

Butchart Gardens, Central Saanich BC

128

Shakespearean Gardens, Stratford ON

Rejoice in Community

Ceilings

The ceiling in your outdoor room will give you the sense of being in a real room and will shade you from the hot summer sun. Overhead built structures such as a porch, a pergola planted with vines, or a gazebo attached to your patio provide permanent shade. They will also allow you to enjoy the outdoors when it's raining, or barbeque as the snow falls. Be sure to add sufficient height to your overhead structure to accommodate hanging vines. If you want your overhead clearance to be eight feet your structure needs to be a minimum of nine feet high when planted, depending on the vines used. The canopy of a deciduous tree could also provide the illusion of a ceiling. Choose your trees and vines carefully as you do not want to sit on a fallen grape, or enjoy an outdoor dinner only to have a walnut drop onto a guest's entrée! Portable shade can be an awning stretched out from the home or a large patio umbrella. These can be set back when full sunlight is desired.

Furnishings

The range of outdoor furniture is as broad as any budget would permit. While budget is often the first consideration, comfort should be high on the priority list. Take a moment to sit in the furniture you plan to purchase to test its comfort. Many plastic furnish-

Author's Garden, Goderich ON

ings offer economy, comfort, and durability, and can be dressed up with all-weather fabric cushions. Finding old garden furniture at yard and auction sales or thrift stores and giving them new life with a sanding and a lick of paint will fill your patio at very little expense. Synthetic wicker, wrought iron, and aluminum furniture is an investment that will last for

Add decorative elements to your garden room. Concrete or wrought iron artwork hung from walls, planters clustered in corners, and rattan or all-weather rugs laid out on the floor add warmth to your space. Life can be added to plain concrete or wood floors by painting or stenciling on a faux rug. Mosaics of tiles, broken glass, or pottery are

ing is the easiest to use but is the most expensive and needs to be carefully chosen and placed so the area is softly lit. Dimmer switches should be installed. An economical choice is to use soft lighting such as that given by candlelight or kerosene lanterns. Benefits of kerosene lanterns and candles are that they are inexpensive, portable, and supply

Claudette and Robert Sherwood, Goderich ON

Jane and Peter Namink, Goderich ON

many years, but styles may change before your furniture begins to decline. One way to renew the look of such furniture is by having it reupholstered. There is a large selection of UV-rated, waterproof fabric available. Fresh fabric can quickly change a dated look.

welcome adornments for concrete floors as well. All-weather fabric cushions add color and softness to furnishings.

Lighting will extend the time of day your patio will be used. Lighting directly wired into your walls or ceil-

soft lighting. Minor inconveniences include the fact that candles are prone to blow out in even the slightest breeze and need to be inside glass containers. Candles left in the sunlight will melt before you use them as lighting and should therefore be stored away after each use. Extra kerosene, a narrow funnel, candles, as well as a good long-handled lighter should be kept close by in a shaded location. You will need to decide for yourself between cost and ease of use when choosing your lighting.

A patio heater can have a radius of over eighteen feet and allow you to make use of your garden room on cool evenings and early spring and fall days. It is a worthwhile investment for those who enjoy spending as much time as possible out of doors but are not interested in an outdoor fireplace. When the need is to cool off rather than get warm, a fan wired into the ceiling of your room will be a blessing on a sultry summer's day. Portable fans can be used outside and there is even a fan available that hooks up to your garden hose and creates a fine, cool mist.

If the song of birds or the hum of crickets is not enough music to your ears, outdoor speakers will bring your favorite music outside. Outdoor speakers can be left outside in all seasons. There are speakers camouflaged as rocks which can be hidden in the landscaping. Other speakers look similar to regular home stereo speakers but are weather resistant and can be mounted under eaves, or behind foliage.

Hatley Park National Historic Site, Victoria BC

Author's Garden, Goderich ON

While relaxing outside with friends and family is sure to be enjoyed by all, sometimes we may be visited by a host of uninvited guests. Mosquitoes and other pesky insects may invade our space and chase all of our friends indoors. Where possible, a screened-in porch or gazebo is a wonderful addition to a patio. Where that is just not possible, you may wish to burn citronella lanterns or candles to chase insects away. Place a liberal amount of citronella candles about your patio; just one or two will not be sufficient to repel flying pests.

Dining Al Fresco

Whether your garden is a balcony or a sprawling acreage, you have space to cook and eat outside. Small spaces require careful organization, but large gardens will benefit equally from organization. Assemble as many frequently used kitchen items into your outdoor cooking area as possible. No one wants to be removed from the party to go into the kitchen to prepare food or to fetch cooking tools that could have been close at hand.

Outdoor kitchens are a wonderful and convenient option. The outdoor kitchen should be located close to the gathering area on the patio or deck. It is always great when the chef can be cooking alongside the guests. The added benefit is that guests are happy to pitch in with preparation. The ideal outdoor cooking area would have a built-in or slide-in barbeque, an under-counter refrigerator, a small sink, counter surface, and hideaway storage for cooking tools, as well as barbeque and surface cleaners. Barbeques that have a direct connection to gas or propane hookups will make better use of space than one which needs a propane tank below. You will

Deb Johnston and Kurt Halmer, Goderich ON

also not be caught in the middle of cooking a juicy steak only to run out of fuel. Balconies should make use of any space under the barbeque to store cooking and cleaning utensils in sealed plastic containers. The more convenient supplies are, the more often we will be inclined to cook and eat outside. An outdoor kitchen that is located under a porch or overhang will be used for barbequing when it rains or snows as well as on warm, sunny days. Just be sure that the barbeque is not situated directly against the wall or else the wall will need frequent cleaning due to the smoke and grease that comes with barbequing. Fire pits and outdoor fireplaces may also double as cooking locations. Incorporating a pizza and bread oven into your fireplace will allow you to prepare the entire meal out of doors.

It is important to choose materials that will withstand all kinds of weather. Stainless steel, granite, and polished, sealed concrete are ideal counter surfaces. The structure around the barbeque and accessories can be made of stone, stucco, brick, or wood such as cedar or teak. The refrigerator, barbeque, and sink will last longer if they are made from stainless steel. It is important in areas that dip below freezing that the water source is turned off before winter.

Rejoice in Community

Sport and Play

While it's wonderful to chat and relax under the shade of a big, old tree, it's also great to interact with each other through sports. Depending on the size of your yard, some or all of the following sports will fit in your yard. The key to sport areas being used is, again, convenience. The most used sports equipment is the kind that is very easily accessed. A bench with a storage area below will provide seating as well as a convenient hiding place for bocce ball, croquet, and other lawn games. Equipment such as balls, gloves, etc. should be located in containers close to where the activity will be played, or in a garage or shed that has shelves and containers to properly organize sports equipment for easy access. Your sports areas should be located as close as possible to the patio. People like to be with people and are more apt to join in a game if it means they are still close to others who prefer to sit and watch. Staying close by also means you may have a cheering section!

Horseshoes are an easy-to-pick-up game and a couple of pits can even fit well into small yards. A regulation horseshoe game is forty-eight feet long measuring from the back of each pit. The pit itself is six by six foot square. Horseshoes can be left hanging from the post to be picked up at any time to play. A smaller yard can shrink the length between pits as well as the pits themselves. Children or those with less swinging power can step ten feet in front of the pit for their turn.

A golf putting green is also a sure hit for family and friends. Natural putting greens are created using creeping bent grass, a very high maintenance grass requiring watering, fertilizing, and mowing attention several times per week. This grass is also prone to disease and insect infestations, and needs to be carefully monitored. Unless you are willing to dedicate your time to a great, natural green, choose from one of the higher quality synthetic greens. Synthetics have come a long way from your local putt-putt golf and can appear quite natural. A good landscape company can install a synthetic green that is guaranteed for ten or more years and is sure to last many years beyond the warranty period. Look for a green that is made of polypropylene rather than nylon. Nylon will deteriorate fairly quickly and is likely to have fungus problems over time. A polypropylene green filled with coal slag is non-biodegradable and the benefit is that you can speed up or slow down the green by the amount of coal slag you put into it. Keeping a few putters in a container or hanging from the wall of your porch will make it easy to putt in a few while waiting for the steaks to grill.

Volleyball is a fun game for even a small crowd, but putting up the net can be time consuming. Installing permanent post holders will make it quick and easy to put up the net. Dig a hole that is six inches deeper than the ground frost limit in your area and put in a manufactured column form. Wrap your volleyball post with plastic and place in the centre of the form, being sure that it is plumb. Pour in concrete. When the concrete is hard pull out the post. You now have good ground supports for your poles making set up quick and easy. The lawn mower can also ride right over the hole which will eliminate the need to trim around a post. Keep the net and posts in an easily accessible area. The posts can also double for setting up a badminton net.

Softball and soccer games need only a large open area and a couple of pylons for goal posts or wood plates for bases. Once again, having the bats, balls and gloves in a convenient spot is key to whether or not a spontaneous game will be struck.

If you have the luxury of space and enjoy a good game of tennis, build your own court. This area can also

Butchart Gardens, Central Saanich BC

double as a basketball court when you roll up the net to one side of the court. A hard surface driveway will also suffice for a little two on two basketball.

A swimming pool is a neighborhood magnet on a hot day. Indeed, you may have more friends than you realize when the thermometer soars! By following local bylaws for fencing and diligence in child safety, your pool will be a wonderful addition to your garden.

Winter is not a time to completely set aside outdoor activities in our yards. In very cold areas back-yards or ponds can be turned into ice rinks suitable for skating, hockey, and broomball. Sloped areas can be used for toboggan hills and front yards can become the neighborhood's center for the arts when your family gets out creating snow sculptures. The fire pit or outside fireplace is a most welcome place to congregate, get warm, and scarf down some creamy hot chocolate and freshly roasted hot dogs.

137

INDEX

139

Z3-9 p.shade/shade
Meadow Rue *(Filipendula vulgaris)*
Z4-9 sun/p.shade
Strawberry *(Fragaria indica, vesca)*
Z5-9 sun
Baby's Breath *(Gypsophila)* varieties
Z4-9 sun
Rock Rose *(Helianthemum)* varieties
Z5-8 sun
Christmas Rose *(Helleborus)* varieties
Z5-9 sun/p.shade
Wild Phlox *(Heperis matronalis)* Z4-9
sun/p.shade
Candytuft *(Iberis)* varieties Z5-9 sun
Scabiosa *(Knautia)* varieties Z4-9 sun
Russian Sage *(Perovskia atriplicifolia)*
Z5-9 sun
Soapwort *(Saponaria)* varieties Z4-8
sun
Pincushion Flower *(Scabiosa)* varieties
Z3-9 sun
Stone Crop *(Sedum)* varieties Z3-10
sun/p.shade

Annuals

Flowering Cabbage *(Brassica oler-
acea)* sun
China Aster *(Callistephus chinensis)*
sun
Wallflower *(Erysimum)* varieties sun
Sunflower *(Helianthus)* varieties sun
Licorice *(Helichrysum)* varieties sun
Stocks *(Matthiola)* varieties
sun/p.shade
Catchfly *(Silene)* varieties sun

TACTILE PLANTS
Annuals

Chenille plant *(Acalypha hispida)*
bears thick, soft, long (10-25cm)
catkins
Floss Flower *(Ageratum)* sun/p.shade

Love Lies Bleeding *(Amaranthus caudatus)* bears thick, soft, long (45-
60cm) flowering tassels
Cockscomb *(Celosia argentea)* full
sun, Soft, feather plumes
Cockscomb *(Celosia argentea)*
Olympia series full sun, soft, intri-
cately wound flower heads
Echeveria *(Echeveria)* thick, fleshy
often large leaves
Licorice *(Helichrysum petiolare)* soft,
furry foliage
Status *(Limonium sinuatum)* Papery
clusters of flowers
Dusty Miller *(Senecio cineraria)* fine,
downy soft foliage

Trees:

Paper bark Maple *(Acer griseum)* Z 4-8
sun/p.shade has peeling, papery bark
Japanese Maple *(Acer palmatum)* Z 5-
8 sun/p.shade has soft, thin foliage
Paper Birch *(Betula papyrifera)* Z2-7
sun/p.shade peeling, thin bark
Dawn Redwood *(Metasequoia glyp-
tostoboides)* Z5-10 sun/p.shade soft,
fine, feathery foliage, peeling bark
White Pine *(Pinus strobes)* Z4-9
sun/p.shade long, flexible needles,
cylindrical, layered cones
Twisty Willow *(Salix babylonica
var.pekinensis* 'Tortuosa') Z4-9
sun/p.shade curled and twisted
branches, small furry catkins
Corkscrew Willow *(Salix matsudana*
'Tortuosa') Z5-9 sun/p.shade curled
and twisted branches, small furry
catkins
Japanese Umbrella Pine *(Sciadopitys
verticillata)* Z5-9 sun/p.shade thin,
firm, rubbery needles formed in whorls
as the spokes of an umbrella

Shrubs:

False Thread Leaf Cypress *(Chamaecyparis pissifera filifera)* Z4-8 full sun
firm, soft, thread like foliage
Climbing Hydrangea *(Hydrangea
anomola petiolaris)* Z4-8 sun/shade
peeling, papery bark
Hydrangea *(Hydrangea macrophylla,
arborescens, paniculata)* Z 4-9
sun/shade large balls or cylinders of
flowers
Mugo pine *(Pinus mugo pumilio)* Z3-7
sun/p.shade thick, rounded shrub with
waxy, flexible needles
Rhododendron *(Rhododendron)* varieties Z5-9 p.shade/shade thick, leathery, smooth foliage
Yew *(Taxus)* varieties Z4-7 sun/p.shade
fine, small, waxy needles densely
arranged on branches

Perennials:

Yarrow *(Achillea)* Z3-8 full sun has
soft, feathery foliage
Maiden Hair Fern *(Adiantum aleuti-
cam, pedatum, venustum)* Z 4-8 full
shade soft, fine foliage
Wormwood *(Artemisia alba, arborescens, schmidtiana, stelleriana)*
Z4-8 full sun soft, feathery foliage
Plume Flower *(Astilbe)* Z 4-8
sun/p.shade soft, feathery plumes (10-
45cm)
Horse Tails *(Equisetum)* Z3-11
sun/shade rubbery, erect, jointed stems
Gunnera *(Gunnera manicata)* Z7-10
sun/p.shade huge leaves (up to 6'long)
wrinkly, serrated foliage
Hosta *(Hosta)* varieties Z3-8
p.shade/shade thick, leathery foliage,
many varieties with very puckered
leaves

Iris *(Rhizomatous Iris)* Z4-9 sun thick, leathery, strap like foliage

Unicorn Rush *(Juncus effuses* 'Spiralis'*)* Z5-9 sun/p.shade thin, firm, curly foliage

Torch Flower *(Kniphofia)* Z5-9 sun/p.shade large, multiflowered heads of waxy, tubular flowers

Blazing Star *(Liatris spicata, punctata)* Z3-9 sun/p.shade long spikes of soft, feathery flowers

Leopards Bane *(Ligularia dentate)* Z4-8 p.sun/shade large, round, leathery foliage

Honesty *(Lunaria rediviva)* Z5-9 sun/p.shade round, papery seed pods

Scotch & Irish Moss *(Sagina boydii, subulata* 'Aurea'*)* Z4-7 sun thick, mat forming foliage, spongy to the touch

Woolly Sage *(Salvia argentea)* Z4-8 sun/p.shade puckered, soft, furry foliage

Saxifraga *(Saxifraga)* varieties Z2-8 p.shade/shade tight clusters of fine mat forming foliage

Sedum *(Sedum)* varieties Z3-9 sun/p.shade small to large foliage which is thick and fleshy

Hens & Chicks *(Sempervivum)* varieties Z5-9 sun thick fleshy rosettes of foliage, some covered with fine hairs

Woolly Lambs Ear *(Stachys byzantina)* Z5-8 sun soft, furry foliage

Woolly Thyme *(Thymus praecox arcticus)* Z 4-8 sun soft, furry, mat forming foliage

Cattail *(Typha minima)* Z2-11 sun/p.shade dense, velvety flower spikes (this variety non-invasive)

Mullein *(Verbascum olympicum)* Z4-9 sun soft, woolly foliage and flower spikes

Adam's Needle *(Yucca filamentosa, flaccida)* Z5-10 sun thick, leathery, strap like foliage extending in rosette form

Spring Bulbs:

Giant Ornamental Onion *(Allium* 'Globemaster'*)* Z5-10 sun/p.shade large, round flowers clusters 15-20cm across

Grape Hyacinth *(Muscari botryoides, latifolium)* Z4-8 sun/p.shade tight, waxy clusters of flowers, feeling like small grape clusters

Grasses of any variety are textural both for their lineal, fine foliage and for their flower plumes which are either soft or bristly.

Any type of fern will add a multi leafed, fine tactile quality

EDIBLE FLOWERS

Flowering Onion *(Allium)* onion flavor, use in soups, sauces and salads

Angelica *(Angelica)* licorice flavor, use in breads, fish dishes

Queen Anne's Lace *(Anthriscus)* carrot flavor, use in salads, sauces

Snap Dragon *(Antirrhinum)* no distinct flavor, use as garnish

Apple, Peach, Pear, use in fruit dishes

Bee Balm *(Monarda)* minty/citris flavor, use in salads or to make tea

Pot Marigold *(Calendula)* spicy, tangy flavor, use in soups and pastas

Carnations *(Dianthus)* clove flavor, use in desserts

Clover *(Trifolium)* licorice flavor, use in desserts

Bachelor's Button *(Centaurea)* clove flavor, use as garnish

Sweet Woodruff *(Galium odoratum)* nutty, vanilla flavor, use in desserts

Sunflower *(Helianthus)* buds artichoke flavor, use as buds, steam

Daylily *(Hemerocallis)* lettuce flavor, use in salads, stir fry

Gladiola *(Gladiolus)* no distinct flavor, use as garnish

Sweet Pea *(Lathyrus ordoratus)* sweet, pea like flavor, use in salads

Lavender *(Lavandula)* unique flavor, use in custards, ice cream

Rose *(Rosa)* sweet, fruity flavor, use in desserts, jellies and jams, hips can be used in jams

Pansy *(Viola)* wintergreen flavor, use in salads

Lilac *(Syringa)* pungent lemon flavor, use in salads

Nasturtiums *(Tropaeolum)* peppery flavor, use in salads, use seeds as caper substitute

Adam's Needle *(Yucca)* slightly artichoke flavored, use as garnish

SCENTED PLANTS

Trees

Spruce *(Picea)* varieties Z3-8 sun/p.shade fragrant foliage

Pine *(Pinus)* varieties Z3-8 sun/p.shade fragrant foliage

Ivory Silk Lilac *(Syringa reticulata* 'Ivory Silk'*)* Z4-7 sun fragrant ivory flower clusters

Linden *(Tilia)* varieties Z3-8 sun/p.shade fragrant ivory flower clusters

Elm *(Ulmus)* varieties Z5-8 sun/p.shade fragrant flowers

Fruit Trees most fruit bearing trees also have fragrant flowers

Shrubs

Butterfly Bush *(Buddleja davidii)* Z5-9 sun/p.shade honey scented long, clusters of flowers

Summer Sweet *(Clethra acuminate,alnifolia)* Z5-8 p.shade fragrant bell shaped flowers

Daphne *(Daphne arbuscula, burkwoodii, cneorum)* Z5-8 sun/ p.shade highly fragrant white to pink flower clusters

Deutzia *(Deutzia)* varieties Z5-8 sun/p.shade star shaped clusters of pink or white fragrant flowers

Witch Hazel *(Hamamelis)* varieties Z5-9 p.shade/shade spidery yellow to red flowers with spicy fragrance

Rose *(Rosa)* varieties Z3-9 sun old roses are often more highly scented than many new hybrids

Lilac *(Syringa)* varieties Z3-8 sun highly fragrant flower clusters

Cedar *(Thuja)* varieties Z5-7 sun/p.shade fragrant foliage

Snowball Bush *(Viburnum x carlcephalum, carlesii, x burkwoodii)* Z5-8 highly fragrant white to pink ball shaped flower clusters

Vines

Chocolate Vine *(Akebia quinata)* Z5-8 sun/p.shade spicy scented flowers

Sweet Autumn Clematis *(Clematis terniflora paniculata)* Z4-9 sun/p.shade heady, sweet scented flowers

Sweet Pea *(Lathyrus nervosus, odoratus)* Z3-10 sun fragrant white, pink and purple flowers

Honeysuckle *(Lonicera varietiesespe-ically japonica* 'Halliana'*)* Z4-9 fragrant tubular flowers

Wisteria *(Wisteria)* varieties Z4-8 sun large clusters of fragrant flowers

Annuals

Angels Trumpets *(Brugmansia)* Full sun sweetly scented flowers

Heliotrope *(Heliotropium arborescens)* sun/p.shade sweet fragranced purple flower clusters

Stocks *(Matthiola)* sun dense fragrant flower spikes

Tobacco Plant *(Nicotiana)* varieties sun/p.shade tubular shaped tobacco scented flowers

Geranium *(Pelargonium)* varieties sun/p.shade pungent scented foliage

Marigold *(Tagetes)* varieties sun distinctive pungent scented flowers

Perennials

Lily of the Valley *(Convallaria)* Z2-7 p.shade/shade highly scented flower clusters

Carnations/Pinks *(Dianthus)* varieties Z3-9 Full sun clove scented flowers

Cranesbill *(Geranium)* Z5-8 sun/p.shade fragrant foliage

Hosta *(Hosta* 'Royal Standard'*)* Z3-8 p.shade/shade highly fragrant trumpet shaped white flowers

Candytuft *(Iberis sempervirens, umbellate)* Z5-9 sun/p.shade small masses of white to pink fragrant flowers

Iris *(Rhizomatous iris)* Z3-9 sun/p.shade large fragrant flowers

Lavender *(Lavandula)* varieties Z4-9 sun highly fragrant flower spikes

Lily *(Lilium)* varieties Z3-8 sun/p.shade often highly fragrant tubular flowers

Bee Balm *(Monarda)* Z4-8 sun/p.shade fragrant foliage

Peony *(Paeonia)* varieties Z3-8 sun large single or ruffled fragrant flowers

Primrose *(Primula)* Z3-8 sun/p.shade fragrant flower clusters

Thyme *(Thymus)* varieties Z4-9 sun fragrant foliage

Violet *(Viola)* varieties Z4-8 p.shade/shade small fragrant flowers

Bulbs

Freesia *(Freesia)* Z8-10 sun highly fragrant funnel shaped flowers

Bluebells *(Hyacinthoides non-scripta)* Z4-9 p.shade fragrant funnel shaped blue flowers

Hyacinth *(Hyacinthus)* varieties Z4-9 sun/p.shade highly fragrant dense clusters of flowers

Daffodils *(Narcissus)* varieties Z2-8 sun/p.shade fragrant trumpet shaped flowers

Herbs

All herbs have fragrant foliage, flowers or both.

ARK THEMED GARDEN PLANTS
Trees

Horse Chestnut *(Aesculus hippocastanum)* Z3-7 sun/p.shade

Snow Bird Hawthorn *(Crateagus mordenensis* 'Snowbird'*)* Z4-8 sun/p.shade

Dogwood *(Cornus alternifolia)* Z4-8, *(contoversa)* Z6-9, *(florida)* Z5-8, *(kousa)* Z 5-8 sun/p.shade

Dove Tree *(Davidia involucrate)* Z5-8 sun/p.shade

Weeping Pussy Willow *(Salix caprea* 'Pendula'*)* Z5-8 sun/p.shade

Shrubs

Yellow Twig Dogwood *(Cornus sericea* 'Kelseyi*)* Z2-8 sun/p.shade

Red Twig Dogwood *(Cornus alba* 'Siberica Variegata','Kesselringii*)* Z2-8 sun/p.shade

Unicorn Cedar *(Thuja occidentalis* 'Unicorn*)* Z2-7 sun/p.sun

Gooseberry *(Groseille a maquireau)* Z4-8 sun

Bluebird Hydrangea *(Hydrangea macrophylla* 'Bluebird*)* Z5-9 sun/full shade

Swan Hydrangea *(Hydrangea macrophylla* 'Swan'*)* Z5-9 sun/full shade

White Moth Hydrangea *(Hydrangea paniculata)* Z4-8 sun/full shade

Butterfly Bush *(Buddleja alternifolia, davidii)* Z 5-9 sun/p. shade

Birds Nest Spruce *(Picea abies* 'Nidiformis*)* Z3-8 sun/p.shade

Grasses

Porcupine *(Miscanthus sinensis* 'Strictus*)* Z4-9 sun/p.shade

Zebra *(Miscanthus sinensis* 'Zebrinus'*)* Z4-9 sun/p.shade

Bunnies Tail Fountain *(Pennisetum alopecuroides* 'Bunnies Tail'*)* Z5-9 sun/p.sun

Perennials

Goats Beard *(Aruncus dioicus)* Z3-7 sun/p.shade

Ostrich Fern *(Matteuccia pensylvanica)* Z 3-8 p.shade/full shade

Leopard's Bane *(Ligularia dentate)* Z4-8 p.sun/full shade

Woolly Lambs Ears *(Stachys byzantina)* Z 4-8 full sun

Solomon's Seal *(Polygonatum biflorum, multiflorum)* Z4-8 p.shade/full

shade

Hens & Chicks *(Sempervivum)* Z 5-8 Full sun

Red Fox Vernoica *(Veronica spicata* 'Red Fox'*)* Z3-8 full sun

Turtle Head *(Chelone obliqua)* Zone 5-9 sun/p.shade

Catmint *(Nepeta mussinii, sibirica)* Z 3-8 sun/p.shade

Bee Balm *(Monarda)* Z4-8 sun/p.shade

Cat's Cradle Daylily *(Hemerocallis* 'Cat's Cradle*)* Z3-7 sun/p.sun

Tiger Kitten Daylily *(Hemerocallis* 'Tiger Kitten'*)* Z3-7 sun/p.sun

Monkey Flower *(Mimulus cardinalis, lewisii)* Z5-8 sun/p.sun

Horse Tails *(Equisetum)* Zone 3-11 sun/shade (invasive)

Unicorn Rush *(Juncus effuses* 'Spiralis'*)* Z5-9 sun/p.shade

Toad Flax *(Linaria)* Z 4-9 sun

Wormwood *(Artemisia alba, arborescens, schmidtiana, stelleriana)* Z4-8 sun

Spiderwort *(Tradescantia andersoniana)* Z4-9 sun/p.shade

Toad Lily *(Tricyrtis hirta)* Z 4-9 sun/p.shade

Cattail *(Typha minima)* Z2-11 sun/p.shade (invasive)

Annuals

Teddy Bear Sunflowers *(Helianthus annuus* 'Teddy Bear'*)* sun

Elephants Ear *(Alocasia)* sun/p.shade

Whirlybird Nastursiums *(Nastursium* 'Whirlybird'*)* p.shade/shade

Spring Bulbs

Donald Duck Tulip *(Tulipa* 'Donald Duck')* Z2-8 sun/p.sun

Blue Heron Tulip *(Tulipa biflora* 'Blue

Heron'*)* Z2-8 sun/p.sun

Parrot Tulip *(Tulipa biflora)* Z2-8 sun/p.sun

Quail Daffodils *(Narcissus jonquilla* 'Quail'*)* Z2-8 sun/p.sun

Dove Wings Daffodils *(Narcissus cyclamineus* 'Dove Wings'*)* Z2-8 sun/p.sun

BIG, BRASH AND BOLD PLANTS
Trees

Indian Bean Tree *(Catalpa bignonioides, speciosa)* Z4-8 large chartreuse foliage and 1 ½ -2' bean pods

Golden Chain Tree *(Laburnum)* Z5-8 sun long chains of yellow flowers

Saucer Magnolia *(Magnolia x soulaneana)* Z5-9 sun/p.shade large 6" cup shaped flowers

Shrubs

Hydrangea *(Hydrangea macrophylla)* Z5-9 sun/shade large balls of flower clusters up to 9" wide

Tree Peony *(Paeonia suffruticosa)* Z4-8 sun large flowers up to 12" in size

Perennials

Rodgersia *(Astilboides tabularis)* Z5-7 p.shade 3' long foliage

Delphinium *(Delphinium)* Z3-7 sun/p.shade flower spikes up to 3 ½' tall

Foxtail Lily *(Eremurus)* Z5-8 sun yellow and orange flower spikes up to 3' tall

Gunnera *(Gunnera manicata)* Z7-10 sun/p.shade huge foliage up to 6' long

Hibiscus *(Hibiscus moscheutos)* Z5-9 sun large bright flowers up to 8" wide

Hosta *(Hosta* 'Blue Umbrellas', 'Grand Master', 'Zounds'*)* Z3-8

p.shade/shade large, low growing foliage
Red Hot Poker *(Kniphofia)* Z4-9 sun yellow, orange or red flower spikes up to 1 ½'long
Leopard's Bane *(Ligularia stenocephala)* Z4-8 sun/p.shade spikes of yellow flowers 2'long
Lily *(Lilium bellingham_* Z5-8 sun/p.shade large bright flowers on stalks up to 6' tall
Ostrich Fern *(Latteuccia struthiopteris)* Z3-8 p.shade/shade tall foliage fronds up to 6' tall

Grasses
Giant Reed *(Arundo donax)* Z6-10 sun/p.shade bamboo like grass up to 23' tall
Pampas *(Cortaderia)* Z6-10 sun 6' – 9' tall plants with large, fluffy flower plumes
Bamboo *(Phyllostachys aureosuleata)* Z6-10 p.shade/shade plants up to 20' tall
Sugar Grass *(Saccharum ravennae)* Z6-9 sun large flower plumes, plant to 12' tall

Annuals
Love Lies Bleeding *(Amaranthus caudatus)* 2' long crimson, chenille flowers
Caladium *(Caladium 'Red Splash')* 2' long red and green foliage
Canna Lily *(Canna)* 2' long foliage, sometimes striped with large yellow, orange or red flowers
Giant Dahlia *(Dahlia)* class AA bright flowers up to 10"
Elephant Ear *(Xanthosoma sagittifolium)* sun/shade large leaves to 36" long

Bulbs
Flowering Onion *(Allium giganteum)* Z5-10 sun/p.shade 4" round, purple flower clusters
Gladiolus *(Gladiolus grandiflorus)* sun brightly colored large flowers on spikes up to 3' tall

Easy to Handle Seeds
Sunflowers *(Helianthus)* sun varieties up to 11' tall, large flower heads up to 10" in size
Morning Glory *(Ipomoea)* sun/p.shade vine bearing brightly colored flowers
Mallow *(Lavatera 'Silver Cup')* sun pink abundant flowers
Marigold *(Tagetes)* sun small to large plants bearing yellow to orange flowers
Nasturtium *(Tropaeolum)* p.shade/shade low or climbing plants with red to yellow flowers
Zinnia *(Zinnia)* Zenith series sun brightly colored large flowers on 36" stalks

FEEDING PLANTS FOR SONG BIRDS
Trees
Serviceberry *(Amelanchier)* Z3-7 sun/p.shade red berries
Dogwood *(Cornus florida, kousa,mas)* Z4-8 sun/p.shade red berries
Hawthorn *(Crataegus)* Z4-8 sun/p.shade red berries
Crab Apple *(Malus)* Z4-8 sun/p.shade red fruit
Mulberry *(Morus)* Z4-9 sun/p.shade red and black fruit
Flowering Plum *(Prunus cerasifera)* Z4-9 sun yellow and red fruit
Flowering Plum & Cherry *(Prunus americana, avium)* Z3-8 sun/p.shade yellow and red fruit
Mountain Ash *(Sorbus)* Z4-9 sun/p.shade orange or red berries

Shrubs
Bearberry *(Arctostaphylos alpine)* Z2-7 sun/p.shade red to purple berries
Chokecherry *(Aronia)* Z4-9 sun/p.shade black berries
Barberry *(Berberis koreana)* Z3-7 sun/p.shade red berries
Beautyberry *(Callicarpa)* Z4-8 sun/p.shade pink to purple berries
Quince *(Chaenomeles)* Z4-8 sun/p.shade yellow fruit
Dogwood *(Cornus canadensis alba, stolonifera)* Z2-8 p.shade/shade red or white berries
Cotoneaster *(Cotoneaster)* Z5-8 sun/p.shade red berries
Holly *(Ilex x meserveae, serrata)* Z4-9 sun/shade red berries
Juniper *(Juniperus)* Z4-8 sun/p.shade green, blue or brown fruit
Oregon Grape Holly *(Mahonia)* Z5-8 p.shade/shade blue berries
Sumac *(Rhus)* Z3-9 sun/shade red seed clusters
Flowering Currant *(Ribes alpinum, laurifolium, odoratum, sanguineum)* Z2-8 sun/p.shade red to black berries
Shrub Rose *(Rosa gallica, glauca, rugosa)* Z2-9 sun/p.shade orange to red rose hips
Skimmia *(Skimmia anquetilia, confusa, japonica)* Z5-9 p.shade/shade white or red berries
Yew *(Taxus)* Z4-8 sun/shade red berries
Cedar *(Thuja)* Z4-8 sun/p.shade green to brown fruit

Blueberry, Cranberry, Huckleberry *(Vaccinium)* Z3-10 sun blue to red berries
Highbush Cranberry *(Viburnum opulus)* Z4-8 sun/p.shade red berries

Vines
Porcelain Vine *(Ampelopsis)* Z4-8 sun/p.shade pink to purple berries
Firethorn *(Pyracantha)* Z5-9 sun/p.shade yellow or red berries

Perennials & Grasses
All grasses and many perennials left standing during the winter will provide seed for the birds.

FEEDING PLANTS FOR HUMMINGBIRDS
Trees
Golden Chain *(Laburnum)* Z5-8 sun
Magnolia *(Magnolia)* Z5-10 sun/p.shade
Shrubs
Butterfly Bush *(Buddleja davidii)* Z5-9 sun
Quince *(Chaenobeles speciosa, x superba)* Z4-8 sun/p.shade
Rhododendron *(Rhododendron)* Z3-9 p.shade/shade
Lilac *(Syringa)* Z3-8 sun
Weigela *(Weigela)* Z4-9 sun/p.shade

Vines
Clematis *(Clematis)* Z3-9 sun/p.shade
Cup and Saucer *(Cobaea scandens)* Z10-12 sun/p.shade
Honeysuckle *(Lonicera)* Z4-9 sun/p.shade
Mandevilla *(Mandevilla)* Z8-12 sun/p.shade
Passion Flower *(Passiflora)* Z7-10
sun/p.shade
Sunfower vine *(Thunbergia)* Z8-11sun/p.shade
Wisteria *(Wisteria)* Z5-9 sun

Perennials
Columbine *(Aquilegia)* Z3-9 shade
Bellflower *(Campanula)* Z3-8 sun/p.shade
Foxglove *(Digitalis)* Z3-8 sun/p.shade
Daylily   *(Hemerocallis)* Z3-10 sun/p.shade
Coral Bells *(Heuchera)* Z4-8 sun/p.shade
Hibiscus *(Hibiscus moscheutos)* Z4-10 sun
Red Hot Poker *(Kniphofia)* Z5-9 sun
Lily *(Lilium)* Z3-8 sun/p.shade
Penstemon *(Penstemon)* Z4-9 sun
Primrose *(Primula)* Z3-8 sun/p.shade
Toad Lily *(Tricyrtis)* Z5-9 p.shade/shade

Annuals
Allamanda *(Allamanda)* sun
Snapdragon *(Antirrhinum)* sun/p.shade
Bouvardia *(Bouvardia ternifolia)* sun/p.shade
Angels Trumpet *(Brugmansia)* sun
Fuchsia *(Fuchsia)* sun/shade
Gladiolia *(Gladiolus)* sun
Tobacco Plant *(Nicotiana)* sun/p.shade
Petunia *(Petunia)* sun
Sage *(Salvia)* sun/p.shade
Nasturtium *(Tropaeolum)* p.shade/shade

BUTTERFLY FOOD SOURCES
Trees
Redbud *(Cercis Canadensis)* Z5-9 sun/p.shade

Shrubs
Butterfly Bush *(Buddleja davidii)* Z5-8sun/p.shade
Daphne *(Daphne)* Z5-8 sun/p.shade
Honeysuckle *(Lonicera)* Z4-9 sun/p.shade
Rhododendron *(Rhododendron)* Z3-9 p.shade/shade
Lilac *(Syringa)* Z3-8 sun
Spirea *(Spiraea)* Z3-8 sun/p.shade
High Bush Cranberry *(Viburnum)* Z4-8 sun/p.shade

Perennials
Yarrow *(Achillea)* Z3-8 sun
Butterfly Weed *(Asclepias tuberosa)* Z3-9 sun
Tickseed *(Coreopsis grandiflora, lanceolata)* Z3-8 sun
Pinks *(Dianthus)* Z4-9 sun
Purple Coneflower *(Echinacea purpurea)* Z3-8 sun
Ageratum *(Eupatorium coelestinum)* Z5-10 sun
Dame's Rocket *(Hesperis matronalis)* Z3-8 sun
Hyssop *(Hyssopus officinalis)* Z4-9 sun
Lavender *(Lavandula)* Z4-9 sun
Gayfeather *(Liatris cariosa, spicata)* Z3-9 sun
Maltese Cross *(Lychnis)* Z4-8 sun/p.shade
Bee Balm *(Monarda)* Z4-8 sun
Ornamental Oregano *(Origanum lacvigatum)* Z5-9 sun
Russian Sage *(Perovskia)* Z5-9 sun
Phlox *(Phlox paniculata)* Z4-8sun/p.shade
Black Eye Susan *(Rudbeckia)* Z3-9 sun
Pincushion Flower *(Scabiosa)* Z5-9 sun
Sedum *(Sedum spectibile)* Z3-9 sun

145

Ageratum *(Eupatorium coelestinum)*
Z5-10 sun
Dame's Rocket *(Hesperis matronalis)*
Z3-8 sun
Hyssop *(Hyssopus officinalis)* Z4-9 sun
Lavender *(Lavandula)* Z4-9 sun
Gayfeather *(Liatris cariosa, spicata)*
Z3-9 sun
Maltese Cross *(Lychnis)* Z4-8
sun/p.shade
Bee Balm *(Monarda)* Z4-8 sun
Ornamental Oregano *(Origanum lacvigatum)* Z5-9 sun
Russian Sage *(Perovskia)* Z5-9 sun
Phlox *(Phlox paniculata)* Z4-8sun/p.shade
Black Eye Susan *(Rudbeckia)* Z3-9 sun
Pincushion Flower *(Scabiosa)* Z5-9
sun
Sedum *(Sedum spectibile)* Z3-9 sun
Woolly Lamb's Ears *(Stachys byzantina)* Z4-8 sun/p.shade
Brazilian Verbena *(Verbena bonariensis)* Z6-9 sun

Weed Plants
Swamp Milkweed *(Asclepias incarnata)* Z3-8 sun
Queen Anne's Lace *(Daucus carota)*
Z3-8 sun
Joe Pye Weed *(Eupatorium purpureum)* Z3-8 sun/p.shade
Goldenrod *(Solidago)* Z4-10
sun/p.shade
Stoke's Aster *(Stokesia laevis)* Z5-9
sun
Ironweed *(Vernonia)* Z3-8 sun/p.shade

Annuals
Ageratum *(Ageratum)* sun/p.shade
Alyssum *(Alyssum)* sun/p.shade
Scotch Marigold *(Calendula)* sun

Alyssum *(Alyssum)* sun/p.shade
Scotch Marigold *(Calendula)* sun

LARVAL FOOD SOURCES
Trees
Birch *(Betula)* Z2-8 sun/p.shade
Hackberry *(Celtis)* Z3-9 sun/p.shade
Hawthorn *(Crataegus)* Z3-8
sun/p.shade
Walnut *(Juglans)* Z3-8 sun/p.shade
Poplar *(Populus)* Z3-9 sun/p.shade
Plum, Cherry *(Prunus)* Z3-8
sun/p.shade
Oak *(Quercus)* Z3-9 sun/p.shade
Willow *(Salix)* Z4-8 sun/shade
Elm *(Ulmus)* 4-8 sun/p.shade

Shrubs
High Bush Cranberry *(Viburnum opulus)* Z4-8 sun/p.shade

Annuals
Snapdragon *(Antirrhinum)* sun/p.shade
Sunflowers *(Helianthus)* sun

Perennials
Wormwood *(Artemesia)* Z3-8 sun
Violets *(Viola)* Z4-8 p.shade/shade

Weed Plants
Burdock *(Arctium)* Z3-8 sun/p.shade
Milkweed *(Asclepias incarnata)* Z3-8
sun
Stinging Nettle *(Urtica)* Z3-8
sun/p.shade

Grasses
Many wild and ornamental grasses are
food for butterfly larvae

DEER RESISTANT PLANTS

Trees
Fraser Fir *(Abies fraseri)* Z4-7
sun/p.shade
Serviceberry *(Amelanchier)* Z3-7
sun/p.shade
Paper Birch *(Betula papyrifera)* Z2-7
sun/p.shade
Dogwood *(Cornus florida, sericea, kousa)* Z4-8 sun/p.shade
European Beech *(Fagus sylvatica)* Z4-7 sun/p.shade
Spruce *(Picea)* Z3-8 sun/p.shade
Scotts, Black and Red Pine *(Pinus mugo, sylvestris, nigra, resinosa)* Z3-8
sun/p.shade
Douglas Fir *(Psuedotsuga menziesii)*
Z5-7 sun/p.shade
Corkscrew Willow *(Salix matsudana* 'Tortuosa'*)* Z5-9 sun/p.shade

Shrubs
Bearberry *(Arctostaphyllos)* Z2-7
sun/p.shade
Barberry *(Berberis)* Z3-7 sun/p.shade
Boxwood *(Buxus)* Z5-8 sun/shade
Blue Mist Shrub *(Caryopteris)* Z5-9
sun/p.shade
Threadleaf Cypress *(Chamaecyparis pisifera)* Z4-8 sun/p.shade
Pepperbush *(Clethra)* Z5-8
p.shade/shade
Broom *(Cytisus)* Z5-9 sun
Daphne *(Daphne)* Z5-8 sun/p.shade
Forsythia *(Forsythia)* Z4-8 sun/p.shade
Inkberry *(Ilex glabra)* Z5-8
sun/p.shade
American Holly *(Ilex opaca)* Z5-8
sun/p.shade
Chinese Juniper *(Juniperus chinensis)*
Z3-9 sun/p.shade

Mount Laurel *(Kalmia latifolia)* Z5-9
p.shade
Wax Myrtle *(Myrica)* Z1-6
p.shade/shade
Japanese Andromeda *(Pieris japonica)*
Z5-8 p.shade/shade
Spirea *(Spiraea)* Z4-8 sun/p.shade
Lilac *(Syringa)* Z3-8 sun

Perennials

Yarrow *(Achillea)* Z3-8 sun
Monkshood *(Aconitum)* Z3-8 p.shade
Gold Alyssum *(Alyssum)* Z4-9 sun
Windflower *(Anemone)* Z3-8 sun/shade
Columbine *(Aquilegia canadensis)* Z3-8 p.shade/shade
Jack in the Pulpit *(Arisaema)* Z4-9 p.shade
Wormwood *(Artemisia)* Z3-8 sun
Goat's Beard *(Aruncus)* Z4-8 p.shade
Butterfly Weed *(Asclepias tuberosa)*
Z3-9 sun
Plume Flower *(Astilbe)* Z4-8
p.shade/shade
False Indigo *(Baptisia)* Z3-9 sun
Bergenia *(Bergenia)* Z3-9
p.shade/shade
Wild Aster *(Boltonia)* Z4-9 sun/p.shade
Siberian Bugloss *(Brunnera)* Z3-7
p.shade/shade
Bellflower *(Campanula carpatica)* Z3-8 sun/p.shade
Turtlehead *(Chelone)* Z3-9 sun/p.shade
Lily of the Valley *(Convallaria)* Z2-7
sun/shade
Tickseed *(Coreopsis)* Z4-9 sun
Pinks *(Dianthus)* Z3-9 sun
Bleeding Heart *(Dicentra)* Z3-9
p.shade/shade
Gas Plant *(Dictamnus)* Z3-8
sun/p.shade
Foxglove *(Digitalis)* Z3-8 sun/p.shade

Purple Coneflower *(Echinacea)* Z3-8
sun/p.shade
Globe Thistle *(Echinops)* Z3-8 sun
Barrenwort *(Epimedium)* Z4-9
p.shade/shade
Joe Pye Weed *(Eupatorium)* Z3-8
sun/p.shade
Spurge *(Euphorbia)* Z4-9 sun/p.shade
Meadow Sweet *(Filipendula)* Z3-9
sun/p.shade
Ferns All varieties
Geum *(Geum)* Z5-9 sun
Cranesbill *(Geranium)* Z4-8
sun/p.shade
Baby's Breath *(Gypsophilia)* Z4-9 sun
Christmas Rose *(Helleborus)* Z4-9
p.shade/shade
Coral Bells *(Huechera)* Z4-8 sun/shade
Iris *(Iris)* All varieties Z3-9 sun
Dead Nettle *(Lamium)* Z4-8
p.shade/shade
Gayfeather *(Liatris)* Z3-9 sun
Leapard's Bane *(Ligularia)* Z4-8
sun/shade
Lupin *(Lupinus)* Z4-8 sun/p.shade
Catchfly *(Lychnis)* Z4-8 sun
Plume Poppy *(Macleaya)* Z4-9
sun/p.shade
Mint *(Mentha)* Z3-8 sun (invasive)
Bee Balm *(Monarda)* Z4-8 sun
Forget-Me-Not *(Myosotis)* Z4-8
sun/shade
Catmint *(Nepeta)* Z3-7 sun
Sundrops *(Oenothera)* Z3-8 sun
Peony *(Paeonia)* Z2-8 sun/p.shade
Oriental Poppy *(Papaver orientalis)*
Z4-9 sun
Russian Sage *(Perovskia)* Z5-9 sun
Balloon Flower *(Platycodon)* Z4-9
sun/p.shade
Jacob's Ladder *(Polemonium)* Z4-9
sun/p.shade

Solomon's Seal *(Polygonatum)* Z3-9
p.shade/shade
Primrose *(Primula japonica)* Z3-8
sun/p.shade
Lungwort *(Pulmonaria)* Z4-8
p.shade/shade
Sage *(Salvia jurisieii, lavandulifolia)*
Z5-9 sun
Soapwort *(Saponaria)* Z4-8 sun
Woolly Lambs Ears *(Stachys byzantina)* Z4-8 sun/p.shade
Thyme *(Thymus)* Z4-9 sun
Goldenrod *(Solidago)* Z4-10
sun/p.shade
Periwinkle *(Vinca minor)* Z4-9
sun/shade

Grasses

Most all varieties of ornamental
grasses are safe from deer

Bulbs

Flowering Onion *(Allium)* sun/p.shade
Fritillary *(Fritillaria)* sun/p.shade
Hyacinth *(Hyacinthus)* sun
Daffodil *(Narcissus)* sun/p.shade

BLACK WALNUT RESISTENT PLANTS

Trees

Japanese Maple *(Acer palmatum)* and
its cultivars Z5-9 sun/p.shade
Maple *(Acer)* varieties Z3-9
sun/p.shade
Southern Catalpa *(Catalpa bignonioides)* Z5-9 sun
Eastern Redbud *(Cercis Canadensis)*
Z5-9 sun/p.shade
Red Cedar *(Juniperus virginiana)* 3-9
sun/p.shade
Oak *(Quercus)* varieties Z3-9
sun/p.shade

147

Canadian Hemlock *(Tsuga Canadensis)* Z4-8 p.shade/shade

Vines and Shrubs

Clematis *(Clematis* 'Red Cardinal'*)* Z4-9 sun/p.shade
February Daphne *(Daphne mezereum)* Z5-8 sun/p.shade
Euonymus *(Euonymus fortunei)* varieties Z5-9 sun/shade
Forsythia *(Forsythia)* varieties Z4-9 sun/p.shade
Rose of Sharon *(Hibiscus syriacus)* Z5-9 sun/p.shade
Arcadia Juniper *(Juniperus sabina)* Z4-7 sun/p.shade
Honeysuckle *(Lonicera)* varieties Z5-9 sun/p.shade
Virginia Creeper *(Parthenocissus quinquefolia)* Z3-9 sun/shade
Mock Orange *(Philadelphus)* varieties Z5-8 sun/p.shade
Multi-floral Rose *(Rosa multiflora)* Z5-9 sun
Black Raspberry *(Rubus occidentalis)* Z5-8 sun/p.shade
Cedar *(Thuja)* varieties Z5-9 sun
Grape *(Vitis)* 4-9 sun/p.shade

Annual

Pot-marigold *(Calendula officinalis* 'Nonstop'*)* sun
Begonia *(Begonia)* fibrous cultivars sun/shade
Morning Glory *(Ipomoea* 'Heavenly Blue'*)* sun
Pansy *(Viola)* p.shade/shade
Zinnia *(Zinnia)* species sun

Vegetables

Squashes, Melons, Beans, Carrots, Corn

Fruit Trees

Cherry, Peach, Plum *(Prunus)* varieties Z3-10 sun
Pear *(Pyrus)* varieties Z4-9 sun

Herbaceous Perennials

Bugleweed *(Ajuga reptans)* 3-8 sun/shade
Hollyhock *(Alcea rosea)* Z3-9 sun
Jack-in-the-Pulpit *(Arisaema triphyllum)* Z4-9 p.shade
Wild Ginger *(Asarum europaeum)* Z4-8 p.shade/shade
Astilbe *(Astilbe)* varieties Z4-9 sun/shade
Lady Fern *(Athyrium)* Z4-9 p.shade/shade
Bellflower *(Campanula latifolia)* Z4-9 sun/p.shade
Dutchman's Breeches *(Dicentra cucullaria)* Z4-8 p.shade
Leopard's-Bane *(Doronicum)* varieties Z4-8 sun/p.shade
Crested Wood Fern *(Dryopteris affinis* 'cristata'*)* Z6-8 p.shade/shade
Sweet Woodruff *(Galium odoratum)* Z5-8 sun/shade
Cranesbill *(Geranium sanguineum)* Z4-8 sun/shade
Grasses
Jerusalem Artichoke *(Helianthus tuberosus)* Z4-9 sun
Coral Bells *(Heuchera* x *brizoides)* Z4-8 sun/shade
Hosta *(Hosta)* varieties Z3-8 p.shade/shade
Siberian Iris *(Iris sibirica)* Z4-9 sun/p.shade
Bee Balm *(Monarda didyma)* Z4-9 sun/p.shade
Sweet Cicely *(Myrrhis odorata)* Z3-7 sun

Sundrops *(Oenothera fruticosa)* Z4-8 sun
Senstitive Fern *(Onoclea sensibilis)* Z4-9 p.shade/shade
Cinnamon Fern *(Osmunda cinnamomea)* Z4-8 sun/shade
Summer Phlox *(Ohlox paniculata)* Z4-8 sun/p.shade
Mayapple *(Podophyllum peltatum)* Z4-9 p.shade/shade
Jacob's-Ladder *(Polemonium reptans)* Z4-8 sun/p.shade
Solomon's-Seal *(Polygonatum commutatum)* Z3-9 p.shade/shade
Primrose *(Primula* x *polyanthus)* Z5-9 sun/p.shade
Lungwort *(Pulmonaria)* species Z4-8 p.shade/shade
Bloodroot *(Sanguinaria canadensis)* Z3-9 p.shade/shade
Golden Stonecrop *(Sedum acre)* Z4-9 sun/p.shade
Showy Sedum *(Sedum spectabile)* Z4-9 sun/p.shade
Lamb's-Ear *(Stachys byzantina)* Z4-8 sun
Nodding Trillium *(Trillium cernuum)* Z6-9 p.shade/shade
Wake-Robin *(Trillium grandifloru)* Z5-8 p.shade/shade
Big Merrybells *(Uvularia grandiflora)* Z3-7 p.shade/shade
Horned Violet *(Viola cornuta)* Z7-9 sun/p.shade
Woolly Blue Violet *(Viola sororia)* Z4-8 sun/p.shade

Spring Bulbs

Glory-of-the-Snow *(Chionodoxa luciliae)* sun/p.shade
Crocus *(Crocus)* varieties sun/p.shade
Winter Aconite *(Eranthis hyemalis)*

148

sun/p.shade
Snowdrop (*Galanthus nivalis*)
sun/p.shade
Common Hyacinth (*Hyacinthus Orientalis* 'City of Haarlem') sun
Grape Hyacinth (*Muscari botryoides*)
sun/p.shade
Siberian Squill (*Scilla sibirica*)
sun/p.shade
Tulips (*Tulipa Darwin, Greigii*) sun

SALT TOLERANT TREES
Hedge Maple (*Acer campestre*) Z5-8
sun/p.shade
Sycamore Maple (*Acer pseudoplatanus*) Z4-7 sun/p.shade
Horsechestnut (*Aesculus hippocastanum*) Z3-8 sun/p.shade
Paper Birch (*Betula payrifera*) Z2-7
sun/p.shade
Gray Birch (*Betula populifolia*) Z3-7
sun/p.shade
Catalpa (*Catalpa speciosa*) Z4-8 sun
Hackberry (*Celtis laevigata*) Z5-9 sun
Hawthorn (*Crataegus x lavallei*) Z5-8
sun
White Ash (*Fraxinus Americana*) Z5-9
sun
European Ash (*Fraxinus excelsior*) Z5-9 sun
Green Ash (*Fraxinus pennsylvanica*)
Z4-9 sun
Ginkgo (*Ginkgo biloba*) Z5-9 sun
Honey Locust (*Gleditsia triacanthos*)
Z3-7 sun/p.shade
Sunburst Locust (*Gleditsia triacanthos* 'Sunburst') Z3-7 sun/p.shade
Kentucky Coffee (*Gymnocladus dioica*) Z5-9 sun
Black Walnut (*Juglans nigra*) Z5-9
sun/p.shade
Eastern Red Cedar (*Juniperus virginiana*) Z3-9 sun/p.shade
Larch (*Larix deciduas*) Z3-6
sun/p.shade
Sweetgum (*Liquidambar styraciflua*)
Z5-9 sun
Magnolia (*Magnolia grandiflora*) Z6-9
sun/p.shade
Black Gum (*Nyssa sylvatica*) Z5-9
sun/p.shade
Colorado Spruce (*Picea pungens*) Z3-8
sun
Austrian Pine (*Pinus nigra*) Z5-8 sun
Longleaf Pine (*Pinus palustris*) Z7-9
sun
Black Pine (*Pinus thunbergiana*) Z5-8
sun
White Poplar (*Populus alba*) Z4-9 sun
Black Cherry (*Prunus serotina*) Z3-8
sun
Oak (*Quercus*) varieties Z3-9
sun/p.shade
Black Locust (*Robinia pseudoacacia*)
Z4-9 sun
Purple Robe Locust (*Robinia pseudoacacia* 'Purple Robe') Z4-9 sun
Weeping Willow (*Salix alba*) Z5-9
sun/p.shade
Corkscrew Willow (*Salix matsudana* 'Tortuosa') Z5-9 sun/p.shade
Japanese Pagoda (*Sophora japonica*)
Z5-9 sun/p.shade
Ivory Silk Lilac (*Syringa reticulata* 'Ivory Silk') Z5-9 sun
Bald Cypress (*Taxodium distichum*)
Z5-10 sun

WINTER INTEREST PLANTS
Trees
Paperbark Maple (*Acer griseum*) Z4-8
sun peeling orange/brown bark
Striped Maple (*Acer pensylvanicum*)
Z3-7 sun/p.shade orangey bark with
white striations
Black Birch (*Betula nigra*) Z4-9
sun/p.shade peeling red/brown bark
aging to black white
Paper Birch (*Betula papyrifera*) Z2-7
sun/p.shade white peeling bark
Weeping Birch (*Betula pendula*) Z2-7
sun/p.shade weeping branches
Weeping False Cypress (*Chamaecyparis nootkatensis* 'Pendula') Z4-7 sun
long pendulous evergreen branches
Hawthorn (*Crataegus*) varieties Z3-8
sun red to black berries
Kashmir cypress (*Cupressus torulosa* 'Cashmeriana') Z5-9 sun fine weeping
evergreen branches
Weeping Beech (*Fagus sylvatica pendula*) Z5-7 sun/p.shade weeping
branches
Beech (*Fagus*) varieties Z5-7 browned
foliage persisting most of the winter
Crape Myrtle (*Lagerstroemia fauriei, indica*) Z6-9 sun peeling red/brown
bark
Crab Apple (*Malus*) varieties Z4-8 sun
red fruit
Dawn Redwood (*Metasequoia glyptostroboides*) Z5-10 sun apricot/brown
peeling bark
Weeping Mulberry (*Morus alba* 'Pendula') Z4-8 sun very twisted branch
pattern
Weeping White Pine (*Pinus strobus* 'Pendula') Z4-9 sun soft foliage evergreen weeping branches
Contorted White Pine (*Pinus strobus* 'Contorta') Z4-9 sun twisted needles
on twisted branches
London Plane (*Platanus*) varieties Z5-9 sun camouflage like peeling bark
Bur Oak (*Quercus macranthera*) Z5-8
sun spurred branches

Pyramid Oak *(Quercus robur fastigiata)* Z5-8 sun columnar tree with browned foliage persisting till spring
Sumac *(Rhus typhina)* Z3-8 sun/p.shade large red chenille seed heads (invasive)
Corkscrew Willow *(Salix matsudana 'Totuosa')* Z4-8 sun upright twisted branches
Bald Cypress *(Taxodium distichum)* Z5-10 sun orange/brown fissured bark
Weeping Elm *(Ulmus glabra 'Camperdownii')* Z5-7 sun twisted weeping branches

Shrubs

Barberry *(Berberis)* varieties Z5-9 sun/p.shade orange to red berries semi evergreen foliage
Red Twig Dogwood *(Cornus alba)* Z2-8 sun/shade red stems
Yellow Twig Dogwood *(Cornus stolonifera 'Flaviramea')* Z2-8 sun/p.shade yellow stems
Cotoneaster *(Cotoneaster)* varieties Z4-9 sun/shade red or orange berries
Euonymus *(Euonymus fortunei, radicans, japonicus)* Z4-9 sun/shade green or variegated evergreen foliage
Wintergreen *(Gaultheria)* varieties Z3-9 sun/p.shade white or red berries
Witch Hazel *(Hamamelis)* varieties Z5-9 p.shade yellow or red spidery blossoms in winter
Hydrangea *(Hydrangea)* varieties Z4-9 sun/shade large dried flower heads
Holly *(Ilex)* varieties Z5-9 sun/p.shade red berries evergreen foliage
Winterberry *(Ilex verticillata)* Z5-8 sun/p.shade profuse red berries no foliage
Kerria *(Kerria japonica)* Z4-9

sun/p.shade lime green stems
Oregon Grape Holly *(Mahonia aquifolium)* Z5-9 sun/p.shade
Firethorn *(Pyracantha)* varieties Z5-9 sun orange or red profuse berries
Highbush Cranberry *(Viburnum opulus)* Z4-8 sun/p.shade red berries
Adam's Needle *(Yucca filementosa, flaccida, gloriosa)* Z5-10 sun thick sword like evergreen foliage

Perennials

Bugleweed *(Ajuga reptans)* Z3-9 sun/shade red purple green and white evergreen foliage
Wild Ginger *(Asarum europaeum, shuttlewrothii)* Z4-9 p.shade/shade evergreen foliage
Heartleaf Bergenia *(Bergenia)* varieties Z3-8 p.shade/shade leathery green foliage
Globe Thistle *(Echinops)* varieties Z3-9 sun spherical textural seed heads
Horsetail *(Equisetum hyemale)* Z3-11 sun/shade evergreen upright jointed stems (invasive)
Sea Holly *(Eryngium)* varieties Z3-9 sun prickly prominent seed heads
Christmas Rose *(Helleborus)* Z4-9 sun/p.shade mid to late winter blooming
Coral Bells *(Heuchera)* varieties Z3-10 sun/shade green purple gold persistant foliage
Corkscrew Rush *(Juncus effuses 'Spiralis', inflexus 'Afro')* Z4-9 sun/p.shade leafless curling stems
Lavender *(Lavandula)* Z5-9 dried flowerheads, grey/green scented foliage
Prickly Pear Cactus *(Optunia compresse)* Z6-9 sun succulent semi pros-

trate spined foliage
Scotch Moss *(Sagina boydii)* Z5-7 sun/p.shade dark green fine foliage
Irish Moss *(Sagina subulata)* Z4-7 sun/p.shade lime green fine foliage
Stonecrop *(Sedum acre, humifusum, lydium, obtusatum, spurium)* Z4-9 fleshy evergreen foliage
Showy Sedum *(Sedum spectibile)* Z4-9 sun/p.shade dried seed clusters
Hens & Chicks *(Sempervivum)* Z4-8 sun succulent foliage rosettes
Periwinkle *(Vinca minor)* Z4-9 green or variegated evergreen foliage
Pansy *(Viola x wittrockiana)* Z4-8 sun/p.shade blooms in mild winter periods

Grasses

All ornamental grasses provide winter interest with dried back foliage and seed heads. The following have special interest as they either keep their foliage color or have striking stems.
Mondo Grass *(Ophiopogon planiscapus)* Z5-10 sun/p.shade green foliage and berries
Black Mondo Grass *(Ophiopogon planiscapus 'Nigra')* Z5-10 sun/p.shade black foliage and berries
Hardy Bamboo *(Phyllostachys)* Z6-10 sun/shade gold to brown jointed tall stems
Black Bamboo *(Phyllostachys nigra)* Z7-10 sun/shade black stems

Branches for Winter Forcing

Quince *(Chaenomeles)* Z5-9 sun/p.shade
Daphne *(Daphne)* Z5-8 sun/p.shade
Forsythia *(Forsythia)* varieties Z4-8 sun/p.shade

150

Witch Hazel *(Hamamelis)* Z5-9
p.shade
Magnolia *(Magnolia)* varieties Z3-9
sun/p.shade
Fruit Trees *(Malus, Prunus, Pyrus)* varieties Z4-9 sun
Pussy Willow *(Salix discolor)* Z4-8
sun/p.shade
Lilac *(Syringa)* Z3-8 sun

GROUND COVER PLANTS
Steppable Plants
Bugle Weed *(Ajuga reptans)* Z3-8
sun/shade
Creeping Jenny *(Lysimachia nummularia)* Z4-8 sun/shade
Moss *(Sagina)* Z4-7 sun/p.shade
Creeping Sedum *(Sedum)* all low
growing varieties Z3-9 sun/p.shade
Thyme *(Thymus)* Z4-9 sun

Low Plants
Goutweed *(Aegopodium)* Z4-9
p.shade/shade
Sea Pinks *(Armeria)* Z5-7 sun/p.shade
Ginger *(Asarum)* Z4-8 p.shade/shade
Woodruff *(Asperula)* Z5-9 sun/p.shade
Astilbe *(Astilbe* 'Perkeo', 'Snowdrift',
'Sprite'*)* Z4-8 sun/shade
Rock Cress *(Aubrieta)* Z5-7
sun/p.shade
Snow in Summer *(Aerastium)* Z3-7
sun/p.shade
Lily of the Valley *(Convallaria majalis)* Z2-7 p.shade/shade
Bunchberry *(Cornus Canadensis)* Z2-7
p.shade/shade
Wandflower *(Galax)* Z5-8 p.shade
Sweet Woodruff *(Galium odoratum)*
Z5-8 p.shade/shade
Cranesbill *(Geranium sanguineum)*
Z4-8 sun/shade

Ivy *(Hedera)* Z4-10 p.shade/shade
Dead Nettle *(Lamium)* Z4-8 sun/shade
Lilyturf *(Liriope)* Z5-10 p.shade/shade
Mondo Grass *(Ophiopogon)* Z5-10
sun/p.shade
Spurge *(Pachysandra)* Z4-9 sun/shade
Creeping Phlox *(Phlox subulata)* Z3-8
sun
Foam Flower *(Tiarella)* Z3-9
p.shade/shade
Periwinkle *(Vinca minor)* Z4-9 sun/
shade

Taller Plants
Barrenwort *(Epimedium)* Z5-9
sun/p.shade
Daylily *(Hemerocallis)* Z3-10
sun/p.shade
Hosta *(Hosta)* Z3-8 p.shade/shade
Ostrich Fern *(Matteuccia)* Z3-8
p.shade/shade
Solomon's Seal *(Polygonatum)* Z3-9
p.shade/shade
Lungwort *(Pulmonaria)* Z4-8
Shrubs
Bearberry *(Arctostaphylos)* Z7-9
sun/p.shade
Heather *(Calluna)* Z5-7 sun/p.shade
Cotoneaster *(Cotoneaster)* Z5-8
sun/shade
Euonymus *(Euonymus)* Z4-9 sun/shade
Wintergreen *(Gaultheria)* Z4-8
sun/shade
Broom *(Genista)* Z5-9 sun
Juniper *(Juniperus, horizontalis,
procumbens)* Z3-9 sun/p.shade
Grape Holly *(Mahonia repens)* Z6-8
sun/p.shade
Skimmia *(Skimmia)* Z6-9
p.shade/shade

Bibliography

Christopher Brickell, Trevor Cole, Judith D. Zuk – Editors-in-Chief. Readers Digest A-Z Encyclopedia of Garden Plants. Westmount, Quebec, Canada: The Readers Digest Association, 1997

Fisher, John. The Companion to Roses. London, England: Viking Penguin Books Ltd., 1986

Bloom, Adrian. Gardening with Conifers. Willowdale, Ontario, Canada and Buffalo, New York, USA: Firefly Books Ltd., 2002

Verey, Rosemary. The Scented Garden. London, England: Marshall Editions Ltd., 1981

Dugan, Dr. Patrick. Guide to Wetlands. Buffalo, New York, USA and Richmond Hill, Ontario, Canada: Firefly Books Ltd. 2005

About the Book

Almost Eden captures the absolute wonder of the earth and teaches us how we can create a little bit of this wonder in our own backyards. Readers will discover how their garden can be in tune with God's original plan of earthly stewardship and be creative and well designed.

For more information and to order additional copies of *Almost Eden*, please visit www.kimburgsma.ca.

About the Author

Kim Burgsma is an award winning landscape designer, speaker, garden class instructor, and author. She writes a monthly garden column for *Focus Newsmagazine* and received an honorary mention for *Almost Eden* in the 2010 Word Alive Press contest. She has owned her own landscape design company since graduating from the University of Guelph in 2000. Her landscape work, home and gardens have been featured in *Life Style, She, City Woman*, and *Canadian Homes* and *Cottages* magazines as well as the *Toronto Star*.